SPHERE RIG

Other titles in the *Sphere Rights Guides* series:

THE CHILDREN'S RIGHTS HANDBOOK Jenny Levin
THE DISABLED PERSON'S HANDBOOK Jan Luba
THE DIVORCE HANDBOOK Jenny Levin
THE HOMELESS PERSON'S HANDBOOK Andrew Arden
THE LAWYER–CLIENT HANDBOOK Olé Hansen
THE MOBILE HOMES HANDBOOK Linda Pearce
THE OWNER-OCCUPIER HANDBOOK Jan Luba
THE PRIVATE TENANT'S HANDBOOK Andrew Arden
THE PUBLIC TENANT'S HANDBOOK Andrew Arden
THE RACE DISCRIMINATION HANDBOOK Harjit Grewal
THE SEX DISCRIMINATION HANDBOOK Harjit Grewal
THE SINGLE PARENT'S HANDBOOK Jenny Levin and Frances Logan

SPHERE RIGHTS GUIDES

Series Editor: Andrew Arden

THE TIED ACCOMMODATION HANDBOOK

SIOBHAN McGRATH

SPHERE REFERENCE

A Sphere Book

First published in Great Britain
by Sphere Books Ltd 1990

Typeset in Plantin by Leaper & Gard Ltd, Bristol, England
Printed and bound in Great Britain by
The Guernsey Press

ISBN 0 7474 0218 3

Sphere Books Ltd
A Division of
Macdonald & Co (Publishers) Ltd
Orbit House, 1 New Fetter Lane, London EC4A 1AR
A member of Maxwell Macmillan Pergamon Publishing Corporation

Contents

Publisher's Notice

The Law can change at short notice. This book describes the law relating to tied accommodation as at 30 April 1990. You should always check if what it says is still correct.

Introduction

This is one of a number of books dealing with the rights of:

Private Tenants. Weekly, monthly or other periodic tenants and tenants with leases of twenty-one years or less, together with lesser rights of occupation known as licences, in houses, flats or rooms where the landlord is a private individual or company, or some other body whose tenants are not public tenants, and who does not otherwise fall within one of the following classes.

Public Tenants. Weekly, monthly or other periodic tenants, and tenants with leases of twenty-one years or less, together with lesser rights of occupation known as licences, in houses, flats or rooms, where the landlord is a local authority, registered housing association or trust, or a development corporation, and who does not fall within one of the following classes.

Owner-Occupiers. Those who with or without a mortgage have a freehold interest in a house or flat, or a lease of more than twenty-one years.

Occupiers of Mobile Homes. Those living in caravans, houseboats or other moveable structures, whether they own those structures or rent them from other people.

Tied Occupiers. Those who have accommodation in houses, flats or rooms from their employers.

Homeless Persons. Those who do not have a home in

which they have a right to live together with those members of their families they would reasonably be expected to live with.

These books do not cover the rights of individuals who have been living somewhere as husband and wife (whether or not legally married) on a domestic breakdown: see *The Divorce Handbook.*

The law in Scotland and Northern Ireland is different from the law in England and Wales which is described in this book; many of the details of the law are different; there are procedural differences, and in some cases there are actual differences in rights. However, much of the information contained in this book concerns rights which Parliament has given to tied occupiers, and as a general rule when Parliament gives rights to occupiers in England and Wales it will seek to give the same or similar rights to occupiers in Scotland, and sometimes also in Northern Ireland.

As an outline of what may well be available, this book may therefore still be of use to those in Scotland and Northern Ireland, although they should always be careful to check the position independently. Useful places to check are:

Shelter (Scotland)
65 Cockburn Street
Edinburgh EH1 1BU
Tel: Edinburgh (031) 226 6347

Shelter (Northern Ireland)
2 St John Street
Omagh
Co. Tyrone
Tel: Omagh (0662) 44985

The law on housing rights changes frequently. This book describes the law as at 30 April 1989.

This book is an outline of what rights are likely to be available to you, as an occupier of tied accommodation. You live in tied accommodation if you reside in premises provided for you by your employer. This does not include the situation where you are self-employed and your accommodation is directly connected to that employment. For example, if you have an agricultural holding which includes accommodation, your rights are not dealt with in this book; or if you have rented accommodation from which you run your own business which includes accommodation in which you reside, your rights are not dealt with in this book. Chapter 1 gives a fuller definition of what tied accommodation is.

For a number of reasons this book cannot tell you in precise detail the full extent of your rights in every situation. For one thing, what your rights are will always depend on the facts which apply to your housing circumstances, or which apply to a particular housing problem. For another thing, many of the rights described in this book have been granted by Act of Parliament. Even though an Act of Parliament may seem to say one thing, judges may interpret it in a way that seems to a layperson completely different. Then again, exactly what an individual contract of tenancy means, or what was agreed or what actually happened, may not be absolutely certain until a judge has considered it, even if it seems clear enough to you.

It is, of course, quite wrong that people's housing rights should be at all uncertain, whether for these reasons, or because the law changes frequently, or because it seems to you complicated or not to add up to a lot of common sense. It is for these reasons that tenants and other occupiers are often unclear what rights they have, and often frightened to enforce what they think their rights may be, in case it results in them being turned out of their homes.

A related problem is that occupiers often do not know where to turn for advice or help (including legal help) and, when they do, they sometimes feel that even the advisers can't tell them exactly what their position is.

The principal purpose of this series is to try to help people know what may be available to them, rather than to tell them exactly what will or may happen in every given situation. The way the series works can best be described by referring to three stages.

The first stage for someone who has a problem, or who just wants to understand his or her situation, is to know that there is, or at the least that there may be, some right, or entitlement, or even a discretion they may be able to take advantage of, and which may benefit them. This series seeks to encourage that knowledge by describing in outline what is available to what class of occupier in respect of the main problems: security of tenure, paying for housing and disrepair.

The second stage is to claim the benefit of that right, entitlement or discretion. Administrators (or landlords, or others) do not shout aloud about what they are able to do to help, or even always publicize what the law obliges them to do to help. It is necessary to ask, and so far as possible to ask with some degree of confidence and accuracy. The series seeks to take the reader far enough to ask, at least in commonplace circumstances, 'Isn't it your responsibility to do this, or give me that?', 'Surely, I don't have to leave, or pay that high a rent?' Often just asking is enough to produce a solution.

Finally, the third stage is when you are still not getting what you want, or you are unsure of what your exact rights are: the landlord is trying to evict you, wants to raise your rent, won't repair, or the local authority will not help you by forcing the landlord to repair, and so on. It is this stage which cannot be covered by this series, because it would require the description of every detail of the whole body of law or administrative provision governing each subject, and covering every possible situation.

It is for this stage that resort must be had to advice agencies or lawyers. In most areas there are Citizens Advice Bureaux, Housing Aid or Action Centres, community groups providing or organizing legal or informed advice, and lawyers who will provide assistance free of charge or at little cost under the legal aid scheme.

Even at this stage, however, this series hopes to help; partly by encouraging the reader to take advice, partly because even lawyers are often not familiar enough with the problems of the people likely to be interested in the right or entitlement dealt with in this series. They may need prodding to find out or check up on whether 'something can be done'.

The client/reader who can open a discussion with an adviser with the proposition that there is 'probably' or even just 'possibly' something which is relevant, using this book to say what, stands a much better chance of securing appropriate advice or aid than the client who cannot.

Against this background there are a few 'golden rules' which should be followed by anyone who wants to make the most of their housing rights without jeopardizing their security in their own home:

(1) Always seek advice at the earliest possible opportunity, to check both your exact position and your best tactics.

(2) Always keep copies of letters and other documents which you fill in, send or receive. Show them to your adviser.

(3) Always keep a note, written as soon as possible afterwards, of any conversations you have with your

landlord, his or her agents or employees, or representatives of a local authority. Date it, sign it and keep it. Show it to your adviser.

(4) Even if you seem to have the right to do so, do not withhold your rent against something you think you are entitled to, such as works of repair, compensation for damage to your belongings, or a lower rent. Go on paying while you take advice and if necessary obtain a court order which proves what you are entitled to do.

(5) Never quit accommodation, for example, because of a high rent, disrepair or even just because your landlord tells you to do so, unless you definitely have somewhere else you are certain you want to go to and that you are certain you will be able to live in. Always take advice before quitting.

(6) Stand up for your rights. Just because you are your only witness and/or there is nothing in writing does not mean that what you say will be disbelieved. Just because it seems difficult to get what you want, don't forget that a little bit of effort trying to establish your rights can sometimes bring substantial housing gains. So don't assume that everyone else, whether a landlord, or the local authority, is right, or more right than you are, or telling you the truth. Always check by taking informed advice.

Finally, in this book landlords and occupiers are referred to by the pronoun 'he'. The sole reason for this is simplicity.

1: What is Tied Accommodation?

What is tied accommodation?

Tied accommodation is the general term given to housing provided by an employer to his employee, as a direct consequence of the employment arrangement. Not all housing provided by an employer is 'tied'; one person may be both a large landlord and a large employer in an area and the fact that you are an employee and tenant of the same person may be coincidental. As the word 'tied' suggests, there must be some connection between your work and your employment. However, if you live in accommodation provided by your employer there is a strong chance that it is tied accommodation.

The type of accommodation is not as important as the fact that the same person who employs you also gives you permission to live there. What is important is that the property you occupy is linked directly to your employment. The accommodation may be a house, a flat or a room to yourself or you may have to share the accommodation. The employer may be an individual, a partner in a firm, a company, a local authority or other public body.

Examples of people who live in tied accommodation are caretakers in blocks of flats, nurses living in flats or rooms provided by their hospital, shop managers living in a flat above the shop premises, members of the armed forces living in accommodation provided by the services, hotel staff provided with a room in the hotel, etc. In every example of tied accommodation there is a dual relationship where the same people are employer/landlord and employee/tenant.

Do all tied occupiers have the same rights?

No. There are different kinds of tied accommodation arrangements, each giving rise to different rights and responsibilities affecting each type. In order to discover which type of tied accommodation arrangement applies to you it is necessary first to decide whether you live in the private sector, the public sector or whether you fit into the special category of agricultural workers.

This book is divided into sections dealing separately with these three categories. At the beginning of each section, the question of what constitutes each of these sectors is answered. In summary they are:

(a) the private sector; accommodation owned by an individual or an organization and rented to, for the purposes of this book, their employees;

(b) the public sector; accommodation owned by public bodies such as local authorities and housing associations and rented to, for the purposes of this book, their employees or the employees of another public body;

(c) agricultural workers; those people who are employed in agriculture and are provided with accommodation by their employers.

Once you have decided which section of the book applies to you, you will then be able to discover in more detail what your rights and liabilities as a tied occupier are. Some of your rights will be the same as other tenants or licensees in the public and private sectors. Where this is the case you will on occasion be referred to the more general books in this series, *The Public Tenants Handbook* and *The Private Tenants Handbook*, for a more detailed examination of the question.

Is the legal terminology which relates to tied occupiers the same as relates to other tenants?

To a great extent, yes. As far as possible technical language is avoided, or explained where it occurs.

Throughout the book, however, two terms or concepts arise with some frequency; they are status and security of tenure.

What does 'status' mean?

Your 'status' is the categorization given to your rights as an occupier. Names are given to the different types of accommodation arrangement you may have. In the private sector the main distinction for tied occupiers is between service tenants and service occupiers. In the public sector the main distinction is between secure tenants and residential occupiers. These are the labels given to your status. In each section of this book the rights and liabilities of persons with a particular 'status' are examined. In housing law generally there occur frequently the terms tenant and licensee: these too are different forms of status. The difference between a tenancy and licence is an important one to understand in every housing context including that of tied accommodation.

What is the difference between a tenant and a licensee?

A tenancy is the name given to the normal arrangement whereby one person pays money for somewhere to live which belongs to someone else. The person who lives in the premises and pays 'rent' is the tenant. The person who allows them to live in the premises is the landlord. A tenancy gives the occupier control of the premises.

A licence may appear to be similar to a tenancy in that there is an arrangement whereby one person allows another to occupy accommodation for payment. The person living in the premises is called a licensee, the person who gives permission for occupation is called the licensor. However a licence is merely a permission to live in premises; it does not give the occupier full control.

Why is the difference between a tenancy and licence so important?

This is because those who are tenants have in general far greater rights than licensees. This is both because they have control of their premises and also because by statute Parliament has given them extensive rights and protections.

How do I tell the difference between a licence and a tenancy?

The starting point for the answer to this question is the details of the arrangement you have with the person from whom you rent your property. The agreement between you may be in writing or it may be an oral agreement. An oral agreement is one made during one or several conversations. To establish that you have a tenancy four ingredients must be present:

(a) Premises – You must be able to identify the premises of which you have a tenancy. For example you may have a tenancy of a house, a flat or even just a room but whatever accommodation you occupy it must not be moveable. For example, if you agree to live in a hostel and agree that you may be allocated whatever room the hostel management directs, then you do not have a tenancy because there is nowhere you can identify as your own.

Also you cannot have a tenancy of half a room, again because you would not be able to identify which part of the room was yours. Once you are able to identify at least a room which is yours, it is not so important that you may have to share facilities such as a kitchen or bathroom.

(b) Exclusive Possession – You must have the right to exclude anyone you wish from the premises *including* your landlord. In effect the premises must have been turned over to you so that you have full control of them.

In almost every case your landlord will have the right

to come into your premises to inspect for repairs or to read meters, etc. These limited rights of access do not prevent you from having 'exclusive possession', because they are merely rights of access as distinct from a right of using the premises. They are for specific purposes as opposed to a general right to use the premises.

The fact that your landlord has a key to your home does not necessarily mean you do not have exclusive possession. There are many reasons why a landlord should have a key (for example, for access in an emergency). If you have the final say on whether or not he may come into the premises, then you have exclusive possession.

(c) Period of Tenancy – You must have agreed a period of time for your right to occupy the premises. This can either be a fixed number of months or years, or it can be a continuing tenancy from week to week or month to month until properly brought to an end.

For example, if you move into accommodation and agree that you will pay your rent at the beginning of every week and do not say how long you will be staying, you will have a weekly tenancy. If, however, you move into a property on the basis that it will be for a couple of nights and there is vagueness about how long you will stay, it will not be a tenancy. However, if you move in on a vague basis and later decide on a period of time you will stay, the agreement will then become a tenancy.

(d) Landlord and Tenant – There must be identifiable parties to the arrangement. There must be a landlord and there must be a tenant. You cannot be a tenant of no one and a landlord cannot let premises to himself.

If these four elements are present then you will be the tenant of the premises you occupy *unless* there is something special or peculiar about the arrangement, in which case the law will only recognize you as a licensee.

For example, if you are given accommodation by a

member of your family as an act of kindness, or are taken in by a friend and share expenses, then the law may regard the situation as being other than the usual landlord/tenant situation and you may be a licensee, because it is clear that the formalities and consequences of a tenancy were never intended to apply to the arrangement.

In most cases normal renting arrangements will be tenancies. There will always be something 'different' about a renting arrangement which is a licence.

Is rent an essential ingredient of a tenancy?

No, but the absence of rent may be indicative that you have a lesser right of occupation than a tenant. Also, if you have a no-rent tenancy you will have fewer rights than others (see page 16).

What is 'security of tenure'?

Security of tenure is the right to remain in your accommodation even if your landlord wishes you to leave. A tenant has greater rights to stay in his home than a licensee. The different categories of tied occupiers have different security of tenure. For example, a service tenant is more easily able to resist a landlord's application to court for possession than a service occupier; thus there are different levels of security. When you have decided which type of accommodation arrangement applies to you, then it is possible to discover what rights you have to stay in your home.

Are my rights other than security of tenure dealt with in this book?

Yes, in each section the issues of rents, sharing and succession are dealt with. Additionally there are general chapters on repairs and homelessness and, for the public sector, the right to buy.

2: Tenancies in the Private Sector

What is the private sector?
The private sector is the description given to accommodation owned and rented by an individual or an organization which is not a public body (see Chapter 7). For the purposes of this book agricultural workers are dealt with in a separate section as they have special rights, although they are mainly within the private sector.

Do all those who live in the private sector have the same rights?
No. You may be either a tenant or a licensee on the basis of the general principles set out on pages 9–12. Additionally, where your landlord is also your employer, you may be a special type of tenant, namely a service tenant, or a special type of licensee, known as a service occupier.

What is the difference between a service tenant and other tenants?
The main difference is that if you are a service tenant your landlord will have greater rights to regain possession of the premises in which you live because you have less 'security of tenure'. The security of tenure of service tenants is dealt with in Chapter 3.

What is the difference between a service tenant and a service occupier?
The main difference is the purpose for which you have been given accommodation. A service tenant is given a tenancy of his accommodation predominantly so that he has somewhere to live. A service occupier is given his accommodation predominantly so that he may do his job properly.

Am I a service tenant?

The question of whether you are a service tenant is to be answered in two stages. The first stage is to establish whether you are a tenant at all (see pages 9–12).

If you are a tenant, the second stage is to consider whether your tenancy was granted to you *in consequence of your employment*. If so then you are a service tenant.

For example, you may be offered accommodation when you take up employment because your new employer has accommodation available and you need somewhere to live. In this case there is a causal connection between your employment and your obtaining the accommodation and hence you are a service tenant. This situation often arises when you move from one part of the country to another to take up employment. In some cases part of the attraction of a new job is the fact that accommodation is available to rent from your new employer. You will also be a service tenant if your existing employer lets you live in accommodation owned by him.

On the other hand, if you are given work by your existing landlord, or if, coincidentally, your employer buys the property you live in, then, because there is no connection between your work and the way you obtained your home, you will not be a service tenant.

If the accommodation you are offered is directly linked to the job you do, for example if you are a caretaker for a block of flats, then you should also consider whether you are a service occupier (see below).

Do I remain a service tenant if my employer sells the property I live in?

This depends on whether your tenancy commenced before or after 15 January 1989. In Chapter 3 it is explained that the rights of tenants were altered from that date. Those whose tenancy commenced before 15 January 1989 are known as regulated tenants. Those whose tenancies commenced after that date are known as assured tenants.

(a) Regulated tenants: if your employer sells the property to another person or company, who also becomes your new employer, then you will continue to be a service tenant. If your employer sells the property to a person or company who has nothing to do with your employment, then you will cease to be a service tenant.

(b) Assured tenants: unlike regulated tenants it makes no difference who your landlord sells the property to; you will remain vulnerable to the extra grounds for possession available against service tenants. See page 34.

Am I a service occupier?

You are a service occupier if the main purpose of your living in the accommodation provided for you is to carry out your job properly. This depends on two things: first of all what your job is; and secondly whether it is necessary for you to live at or very close to your work in order to carry out that job.

A person who is employed has a contract of employment. This is often, but not always, written down and is a list of the duties and rights of an employee. If the duties included in the contract of employment are of a nature that make it necessary for you to live at or very near to your place of work then you will be a service occupier.

'Necessary' in this context means 'for the better performance' of your duties; it does not mean that your employer simply wants you to live in some particular accommodation which happens to be close to your place of work. It also does not relate to your own personal housing need. Of course it is necessary for everyone to have somewhere to live but this in itself does not relate to the particular duties you carry out at work.

The job and the accommodation must be directly linked; for example, if your job includes being on call in the vicinity of your work at all hours of the day or night then you will be a service occupier. On the other hand, if it is merely a bit more convenient to live near to your work without actually being a part of the job you will probably be a service tenant. For example a 'live-in' nanny will almost certainly be a service occupier, whereas a bank clerk living in accommodation owned by the bank will almost certainly be a tenant or, if he obtained the accommodation in consequence of his employment, a service tenant.

Does it make a difference whether I am paying rent?

Yes. First it is important to note here that 'paying rent' does not have to take the form of handing over cash or a cheque to your landlord. In a tied accommodation arrangement, paying rent can, and often does, take the form of an agreed deduction from your salary or an agreed amount, never shown on your payslip, which is attributable to your accommodation. What is important is that a quantifiable sum of money is agreed between you and your landlord as being payment for your accommodation and that this payment is 'made' at regular intervals.

If there is no agreed amount deducted from your salary or attributed to your accommodation, then it is extremely likely that you will be a service occupier rather than a service tenant. This will only not be true if the actual accommodation, and the job, are completely unconnected. In that case, although you may be a service tenant instead, it will be a 'no rent tenancy' and your rights as a tenant will be very few. See page 36 for your security of tenure. Alternatively if you are paying no rent this may be an indication that you are only a licensee (see pages 9–12).

Even if you do pay rent this does not automatically mean you are a service tenant rather than a service occupier. The main test still applies, and you will be a service occupier paying rent if it is necessary for you to occupy the premises in order to do your job properly.

3: Service Tenants – Security of Tenure

Do all service tenants have the same security of tenure?
No. As a service tenant your rights are, with a few important exceptions, which are dealt with in this chapter, the same as any other tenant in the private sector.

Those tenants who pay rent have far greater rights to stay in their accommodation than those who do not; this is because they have been given protection at law by statute.

If you are a rent-paying tenant and your tenancy commenced on or after 15 January 1989 your protection comes from the Housing Act 1988 and your rights are different from the rights of rent-paying tenants whose tenancies began before that date and who are protected by the Rent Act 1977.

A. TENANCIES COMMENCING BEFORE 15 JANUARY 1989

Do all those whose tenancies commenced before 15 January 1989 have the same security of tenure?
No. The majority of those who have tenancies commencing before 15 January 1989 can broadly be divided into the following categories;

1. Restricted Contract Tenants
Those who have a room or rooms to themselves in accommodation where their landlord also lives are known as restricted contract tenants. For example, if you were employed in a bank and your manager let you rent a room to yourself in his house you would be a restricted contract tenant there. You would still be a restricted contract tenant even if the rented accommodation in your employer's home had its own cooking and washing facilities.

2. Regulated Tenants
Those tenants whose accommodation is in a different building from their employer/landlord's home are known as regulated tenants.

3. Tenants Excluded from Protection
There is also another category of tenant in much the same position as no-rent tenants who do not qualify for protection because they have been specifically excluded. The main exclusions are:

(i) those who pay a very low rent,

(ii) those who live in premises with a very high rateable value, or if obtained after 31 March 1990 the rent exceeded £25,000 a year,

(iii) those who have substantial board (meals) and attendance (cleaning) included in their tenancies,

(iv) those who obtained their tenancy for a holiday,

(v) those who have a tenancy of premises licenced for the sale of alcohol for consumption *on* the premises. This exemption would apply, for example, if you were employed in a pub, and were given rented accommodation on the premises of the pub. Note that the exemption is for on-licence premises not off-licence.

If you are a no-rent tenant or otherwise fall into the list of tenancies excluded from protection set out above, your rights are dealt with on page 35.

What is the difference in the security of tenure of restricted contract tenants and regulated tenants?
The main difference is that regulated tenants have more security than restricted contract tenants. This means that they have more rights to stay in their homes. For both restricted contract tenants and regulated tenants, a landlord must go to court to obtain an order for possession before he can ask them to leave their premises. Also, before a court will give your landlord an order for possession in either case, your 'contractual tenancy' must have come to an end.

What is my 'contractual tenancy'?
The agreement between you and your landlord that you may live in the premises you occupy is known in law as a contract; it is an agreement much like any other commercial agreement. For example, agreements to buy and sell are contracts; agreements to hire are contracts; agreements to work are contracts. The agreement between you and your landlord need not be written down to be valid. While your contract or agreement to live in your accommodation exists, your landlord cannot force you to leave.

How does my contractual tenancy come to an end?
There are various different ways in which your contractual tenancy can come or be brought to an end. A distinction can be drawn between those tenancies which are for a fixed period of time, known as 'fixed-term tenancies' and those which are not for a fixed period of time, which are known as 'periodic tenancies'.

Fixed-term tenancies
If you agreed with your landlord that you would occupy your premises for a fixed period of time, for example for six months, then at the end of that period of time your

agreement will come to an end. Unless you make a new agreement with your landlord that you will continue to live at the premises you will no longer have a 'contractual tenancy'. Fixed-term tenancies may be brought to an end earlier than the date agreed by a process known as 'forfeiture'. A contract is forfeited, that is, brought to an end, if you and your landlord agreed that it would not continue if you acted contrary to the arrangement between you and you did, in fact, so act. This is known as a breach of contract. Examples of breaches are not paying rent or causing a nuisance. Once you have acted contrary to the agreement it is up to your landlord whether or not to treat the contract as coming to an early end. If he decides to ignore the breach, then your contract will carry on until the end of the fixed term. The landlord can only forfeit your tenancy by means of a court order.

Periodic tenancies

If you did not agree a fixed period of time to stay in your accommodation, you have a periodic tenancy. A periodic tenancy is one that lasts for a period of time, usually a week or a month, at the end of which it is automatically renewed. These tenancies are often referred to as 'weekly' or 'monthly' tenancies. A periodic tenancy will only not be automatically renewed from week to week or month to month if it is brought to an end by a positive act by either you or your landlord. The most common way of bringing a tenancy to an end is by a notice to quit.

What is a notice to quit?

A notice to quit is a written document given by your landlord to you (or by you to your landlord), saying that your tenancy will come to an end on a specified date. If you have a weekly tenancy that date must be at least four weeks away. If you have a monthly tenancy that date must be at least a month away. The notice must also contain written information about your right to stay in the premises until a court order is made notwithstanding that your tenancy has come to an end. It must also inform you about your right to legal advice. This information is in a specific form prescribed by Parliament. Without this information the notice to quit will not be valid.

Does my contractual tenancy come to an end if I am dismissed or leave my employment?
No. If you are a true service tenant your tenancy comes to an end or is brought to an end as described above. It is separate from your employment rights. The position is different if you are a service occupier (see pages 36–39).

Must I leave my accommodation once my contractual tenancy has come to an end?
No. You are entitled to stay in your home until an order for possession is made by a court. However, your rights are different depending on whether you are a restricted contract tenant or a regulated tenant.

Restricted Contract Tenants
When your contractual tenancy has come to an end, you are entitled to remain in your home until an order for possession is made against you. This right of 'irremovability' however is the only concrete right you have. Any other right you had under the agreement between yourself and your landlord will have ended.

Regulated Tenants
While your contractual tenancy exists you are known as a 'protected tenant', when it comes to an end you become a 'statutory tenant'. A statutory tenancy is a continuation of the tenancy which has been terminated. All of the rights and obligations of the contractual tenancy are carried over into the statutory tenancy. For example,

your rights to have your home repaired and your rights to share the premises remain the same. A statutory tenancy continues until either an order for possession is made against you *or* you permanently move out of the premises.

How can my landlord obtain an order for possession against me?

Again, this is different depending on whether you are a restricted contract tenant or a regulated tenant.

Restricted contract tenants

All your landlord need do is to prove to the court that you were a restricted contract tenant and that your tenancy came to an end before your landlord applied to the court for possession. Once a judge is satisfied about both of these facts then he has no choice but to make an order for possession.

If your tenancy commenced after 28 November 1980, the judge has the power to postpone the date for possession for up to three months. If your tenancy commenced before that date the judge only has power to postpone the date you must give up possession for a maximum of six weeks. In these circumstances an order for possession is usually made to take effect in 28 days. If you are a restricted contract tenant whose tenancy commenced prior to 28 November 1980, however, you have the right to apply to the 'rent tribunal' when you receive a notice to quit, to ask them to suspend its operation for three months (see *The Private Tenants Handbook* for your rights).

Regulated tenants

Before a court will make an order for possession against you, the judge must be satisfied, first that your contractual tenancy came to an end before your landlord applied to the court for possession and, second, that there is a 'ground' for possession against you.

What are the 'grounds' for possession?

The 'grounds' for possession are specific reasons set out in the Rent Act for the courts to order you to leave your home. The grounds in the Rent Act are known as 'cases'. All of the grounds for possession against a private tenant are available against a service tenant. There is also one additional ground, specifically aimed at service tenants. This ground is not available against other private sector tenants and is dealt with in detail below.

The grounds can be divided into two categories; firstly, 'discretionary' grounds which, if made out, still leave the court with a residual discretion whether or not to grant an order for possession. The residual discretion is that the judge must be satisfied that it is 'reasonable' to order possession against you. Secondly, 'mandatory' grounds which are those grounds which, if made out, leave the court no choice but to grant an order for possession.

What is 'reasonableness'?

This is an overriding factor which requires the judge to consider whether or not to order possession against you. The judge should have regard to all factors relevant to yourself, your landlord and to whichever discretionary ground for possession has been proved.

As far as the ground for possession is concerned, if you are at fault, but the matter is only trivial, for example if you are three weeks in arrears with your rent, or there has been an isolated incident of nuisance, then it would probably not be reasonable to order possession against you.

As far as your own and your landlord's circumstances are concerned, everything is relevant in deciding reasonableness; for example, whether you have been a good tenant and your landlord a good landlord, your family circumstances and your health, your financial circumstances and your landlord's financial circumstances, how long you have been in occupation of your home, etc.

The above considerations apply to all cases of private tenants who have had a discretionary ground for possession proved against them. As a service tenant, the fact that you have obtained your home in consequence of your employment will also be a relevant factor for the judge to take into account. For example, your job performance may be relevant to show whether you are a reliable person or not; or you may have given up other secure accommodation to move to a new job. If you have been dismissed from your work the question of whether the dismissal was fair or unfair may be decisive in the question of whether possession should be ordered against you.

What are the discretionary grounds for possession?

There are nine discretionary grounds for possession. Eight of these grounds are available against all private tenants, the ninth ground is specifically aimed at service tenants. The eight grounds which apply to all tenants, including service tenants, can be divided into two types: grounds which involve fault on the part of the tenants, and grounds which involve no fault.

What are the grounds which involve fault on the part of the tenant?

These include: rent arrears, breach of a term of a tenancy, nuisance and annoyance to adjoining occupiers, damage to premises or furniture provided by a landlord and illegal or immoral use of the premises.

There is also a ground where you have given a valid notice to quit to your landlord and he has arranged to let the premises to someone else or sell the property and you have decided not to go.

If your tenancy agreement forbids you to sublet (i.e. to rent out the premises to someone else) either the whole or part of the premise, and you do so, this is also a ground for possession.

Finally, if there is a rent registered for the premises (see page 43) and you charge a subtenant more than is permitted, this is also a ground for possession.

What are the grounds which involve no fault on the part of the tenant?

There are two grounds which fall into this category, other than the one relating to service tenants. The first is that your landlord requires the premises either for himself or one of a specified list of relations (children over 18, parents or parents-in-law) to live in. The requirement must be reasonable. Also it is not available to a landlord who bought the premises whilst you were living in it. The judge must also consider whether greater hardship would be caused to you if an order for possession were made on this ground, or to the landlord if no order for possession were made. Finally the judge must also make a decision on the question of reasonableness (see page 24).

The second ground is that suitable alternative accommodation is available to you. The alternative accommodation must be suitable in the sense that it is big enough for you and your family, near enough to your work and subject to as much security of tenure as your present home. Also the premises must be similar to your present accommodation or otherwise suitable, as regards 'character'. For example, a letting of a flat above a chip shop is no substitute for a house in a quiet residential street. Finally the alternative accommodation must be suitable as regards rent.

What are the mandatory grounds for possession?

Altogether there are ten mandatory grounds for possession set out in the Rent Act. All of the grounds are applicable to service tenants as they are to other regulated tenants.

Four grounds relate to property which has been occupied at some time in the past by ministers of religion or people employed in agriculture and are rarely used nowadays. A further ground relates to an out-of-season letting sometimes called a 'winter let'. This must be for a fixed term of not more than eight months, and written notice of the ground be given before the letting. Another ground relates to property usually let by specified educational institutions to students. This may be let for a fixed term of not more than twelve months, again with the tenant having been given written notice.

Two of the remaining grounds are more commonly used. They are:

(a) A ground to benefit temporarily absent 'owner occupiers'. To establish this ground the property must have been occupied by the landlord as a residence. The landlord must have given any tenants of the property written notice that he may wish to return to the property, and notice that he would rely on this ground to obtain possession. He must also prove that he does wish to return to the property.

(b) A ground to benefit those who own retirement homes. Here written notice of an intention to use this ground must have been given to any tenant the property was let to. The owner must also show he has retired and wishes to reside in the property.

Finally there are grounds to assist members of the armed forces who let out property, and one confined to lettings on 'shorthold' tenancies. This latter type of tenancy is not dealt with in this book and if necessary reference should be made to *The Private Tenants Handbook*.

What is the ground for possession specifically aimed at service tenants?

This is a discretionary, no-fault ground, and only applies

when you have been dismissed or have left your employment. Your landlord must show that he requires your accommodation for another employee and can prove:

(a) that at the time you commenced occupation of the accommodation you were employed by him;

(b) that you obtained the accommodation as a result of your employment. In other words your landlord would not have let you the accommodation if you hadn't been his employee. It makes no difference whether you knew that your landlord had this motive or not. Also it makes no difference if you didn't know that once your employment ended your employer would want the accommodation back;

(c) that your employment has ended. It does not matter how your employment has come to an end; you may have been dismissed or have resigned. Even if you have been wrongfully or unfairly dismissed your landlord can still probably rely on this ground;

(d) that he reasonably requires the accommodation for another employee. Your landlord needs to show that there is another person who is already employed by him for whom he needs the accommodation. He must also show that his requirement is reasonable, i.e. not merely a device to obtain a court order against you. For example, if he had several other suitable empty properties in which the other employee could live, his requirement would not be reasonable;

(e) that it is reasonable to make an order for possession against you. This is the reasonableness mentioned on page 24 and is in addition to your landlord showing that he reasonably requires the premises.

Does it make any difference if I was unfairly or wrongfully dismissed from my employment?

Yes. The ground for possession itself is still available to your landlord but you may be able to persuade the judge in the case that the way in which you were dismissed makes it unreasonable to order possession against you. Also if you have applied to an industrial tribunal for a ruling on your dismissal you may be able to persuade the court to postpone the possession proceedings until the industrial tribunal's decision is known. If the industrial tribunal orders your reinstatement or re-engagement then it may be arguable that this specific ground for possession then ceases to apply to you.

If the court decides to make an order for possession against me when must I leave?

This depends on whether the court has ordered possession on the basis of a mandatory or a discretionary ground. The rules relating to service tenants are the same as those relating to other tenants in the private sector:

(a) Mandatory grounds: In these cases the court has a general power to postpone the date for possession for such period as it sees fit. There must be a final date given for possession, and in the absence of special circumstances a period of four weeks is usually given before the order comes into effect.

(b) Discretionary grounds: For discretionary grounds the court has much wider powers. Firstly, it may order possession at any date in the future. In many cases four weeks is what is given in practice.

Secondly, the court may not make an outright order for possession, but instead make a 'suspended' order. This means that the court imposes certain conditions on the tenant which he must abide by. If he does not comply with the conditions then the order for possession may be brought into effect by the landlord. For example, if there are rent arrears the court may provide that the arrears be paid off in instalments, or if there has been nuisance and annoyance that the cause of the nuisance be abated. So long as the terms of the suspended order are complied with, possession may not be recovered. If a suspended order for possession is made against you, you should be careful to try and ensure that it is limited in time and that after that period of time it is automatically discharged.

Thirdly, if an order for possession, whether suspended or not, has been made against you, you may apply to the court to have the date for possession postponed, or the terms of a suspended order varied or discharged. For example if you have been ordered to pay off your rent arrears at a particular rate, but later your circumstances change and you can no longer afford to pay at that rate, then you can make an application to pay less.

B. TENANCIES COMMENCING ON OR AFTER 15 JANUARY 1989

Do all those whose tenancies commenced on or after 15 January 1989 have the same security of tenure?

No. The majority of those who pay rent and who have tenancies commencing on or after 15 January 1989 can broadly be divided into the following categories:

1. Excluded Tenancies

Those who have a room or rooms to themselves in accommodation where their landlord also lives have what are known as *excluded tenancies.* Unlike pre-15 January 1989 tenancies, these enjoy no special protection and are dealt with at the end of this chapter under the heading of tenancies with no special protection (see page 35).

2. Assured Tenancies

Those whose accommodation is in a separate building from their landlord or in a purpose-built flat are known as *assured tenants.*

3. Tenancies Excluded from Protection
There is also another category of tenant in much the same position as no-rent tenants and who do not qualify for protection because they have been specifically excluded. The exclusions are similar to those listed on page 19 in relation to regulated tenants. The main differences are that those who have board and attendance included in their tenancies are not specifically excluded from being assured tenants, and that if you obtained the tenancy after 31 March 1990, the rent is less than £1,000 in London or £250 elsewhere.

How can my landlord obtain an order for possession against me if I am an assured tenant?
In most cases your landlord will have to prove two things. Firstly, that he has served a valid 'notice of proceedings for possession' on you and, secondly, that there are grounds for possession. In addition to some ground for possession, your landlord will have to show that it is reasonable to make an order for possession.

What is a 'notice of proceedings for possession'?
This is a notice set out in an official format which warns you that your landlord is intending to take you to court to get possession of your home. In short, it gives you a date after which the proceedings may be begun and the grounds or reasons on which your landlord will base his request to give him his order for possession. The minimum period after which your landlord can start possession proceedings is two weeks after the notice has been served on you. For certain grounds that period is extended up to two months, or, if longer, the same period as a notice to quit (see above, page 21). If your landlord has now served you with one of these notices he can still ask the court to make an order for possession against you, but only if he can show that it is 'just and equitable' for the court

to do so, i.e. that it is fair to do so. For example, if the case is very urgent and your landlord has let you know he was going to take proceedings and why, then that may be enough.

What are the 'grounds for possession'?
Grounds for possession are the reasons set out in statute for the court to order you to give up possession of your home. All of the grounds available against assured private sector tenants are available against assured service tenants. As with pre-January 15 1989 tenancies, these grounds can be divided into two types, mandatory and discretionary. *Mandatory grounds* are those which, if proved, leave the court no choice but to make an order for possession. *Discretionary grounds*, if proved, leave the court with a residual discretion to decide whether it is reasonable to make an order for possession against you (for the meaning of reasonableness see page 24).

What are the mandatory grounds for possession?
Altogether there are eight mandatory grounds. Four of the grounds are cases where the tenant must have been given notice not later than the beginning of the tenancy that possession may be recovered on the basis of those grounds. They are:

(a) that the landlord occupied the premises prior to the tenancy as his only or principal home and that he again requires the premises either for himself or his spouse, as their only or principal home;

(b) that the tenancy is for a fixed period not exceeding eight months and that at some time during the twelve months immediately preceding the tenancy it was occupied for the purpose of a holiday;

(c) that the tenancy is for a fixed period not exceeding twelve months and that at some time during the twelve months immediately preceding the tenancy it was occupied as a student letting;

(d) that the premises are held for the purpose of being available for occupation by a minister of religion as a residence from which to perform the duties of his office, and that it is required by a minister of religion as such a residence.

The remaining four which do not require notice to have been given are:

(e) that the premises are subject to a mortgage or charge and that the mortgagee requires possession of the premises in order to sell;

(f) that the landlord (who must not have purchased the premises during the currency of the tenancy) intends to demolish or reconstruct or carry out substantial works on the premises and the work cannot be carried out with the tenant in occupation and that *either*:

(i) the tenant is not willing to give access or otherwise facilitate the works, *or*

(ii) the nature of the works prevents the tenant from remaining in occupation, *or*

(iii) the tenant refuses to accept a tenancy of part of the premises which would allow the works to be carried out, *or*

(iv) the nature of the works is such that no tenancy of such a part could be offered;

(g) that the tenant has died and within twelve months after the death of the tenant possession proceedings are begun.

(h) that both at the date of the notice of proceedings for possession and at the date of the court hearing there are at least three months' rent arrears.

What are the discretionary grounds for possession?

There are eight discretionary grounds. Six of these involve some fault on the part of the tenant. They are: rent arrears, persistent delay in paying rent, other obligations under the tenancy have been broken (e.g. repairs), damage to the premises, nuisance and annoyance to neighbouring occupiers and damage to furniture.

Of the other two discretionary grounds, one is that suitable alternative accommodation is available. This ground is in substance the same as that available against regulated tenants (see page 26). The other ground is directed specifically to service tenants.

What is the ground specifically directed to service tenants?

The ground is that your home was let to you in consequence of your employment and that you have been dismissed from or left your employment.

The ground applies only if your accommodation was let to you by your landlord as a result of your employment with him, i.e. if you hadn't been employed by your landlord you would not have been given the accommodation. This ground is also available to a new landlord who has taken over from your original landlord, even if the new landlord does not also employ you. This ground is one for which the court also has to be satisfied that it is reasonable to make an order for possession against you. Therefore all the information you and your landlord put before the court about yourselves and the tenancy will be taken into account before the judge decides whether or not to give an order for possession. If you were unfairly or wrongfully dismissed from your employment then the arguments set out on pages 28–29 also apply to you.

If an order for possession is made against me, when must I leave?

The answer to this question is the same as for tenancies commencing before 15 January 1989, see page 29.

C. TENANCIES WITHOUT SPECIAL PROTECTION

Does my landlord have to go to court to obtain an order for possession against me?

In most cases, yes. However there is one important exclusion, that is where you have a tenancy which commenced after 15 January 1989 and you live in the same building or flat as your landlord, i.e. you have an excluded tenancy: in such a case, the landlord need not use court proceedings to evict you once your tenancy has come to an end. In this category there is no statutory requirement for your landlord to include the prescribed information described on page 22 when he serves you with a notice to quit.

What does my landlord have to prove to the court?

All that your landlord need prove to the court is that your contractual tenancy has come to an end. See pages 20–21 for how this may be achieved.

Once it has been proved to the court that your contractual tenancy has come to an end, the judge has no choice but to make an order for possession against you.

Do I have to leave the premises as soon as an order for possession is made against me?

No, the judge in the case will set a date for possession which will usually be fourteen days after the hearing but in cases of great hardship can be as much as six weeks.

If you wish to seek rehousing from your local authority, you should not normally leave your accommodation before a court order has been obtained against you. See Chapter 19 and page 103.

4: Service Occupiers – Security of Tenure

Do all service occupiers have the same security of tenure?
No. There are some differences depending on whether or not you share the premises with your landlord. For all service occupiers, however, security of tenure is limited. Once your employer/landlord has withdrawn his permission for you to reside in the accommodation provided for you then his regaining possession of that accommodation is inevitable.

How can my landlord withdraw permission for me to live in my accommodation?
There are two main ways in which permission can be withdrawn from a service occupier to live in his accommodation; first, as a service occupier your right to occupy your premises is connected to your contract of employment. If you are dismissed or resign from your job then your contract of employment is brought to an end and your right to live in your premises is also brought to an end.

If you are dismissed from your employment you are usually entitled to a period of notice that your employment will come to an end. Unless your contract of employment gives you the right to a longer period of notice this is one week for each year you have been in your employment and you are entitled to at least the same period of notice from your landlord that you must leave your accommodation. Additionally it is arguable that as you are a form of licensee (see page 9) you are entitled to 'reasonable notice' that your right to occupy the premises will come to an end. In some circumstances this period may be longer than the period you are entitled to under your contract of employment (see below).

Secondly, it is possible that your landlord wishes to withdraw his permission for you to live at your premises without affecting your employment rights. This would be an unusual situation since to be a service occupier it must be *necessary* for you to live at the premises to carry out your work (see page 15). However, such a situation is not inconceivable; for example, your landlord may wish only to move you to live in premises adjacent to those you already occupy. In such a case your landlord may withdraw his permission for you to occupy your home by giving you 'reasonable notice'.

What is 'reasonable notice'?

The question of whether the amount of notice you have been given is reasonable or not depends on your individual circumstances, for example the length of your employment, the reasons for the notice, the time spent living in the accommodation, the type of accommodation, the type of job you do, your relationship with your employer, etc. For example, an occupier who has children and who loses his job through no fault of his own will probably be entitled to more notice than an occupier who has no dependants and has been dismissed for gross misconduct such as theft from his employer.

As a guide, twenty-eight days notice is frequently regarded as being reasonable (also see below as to requirement for formal notice). However, if the period of the notice you are entitled to under your contract of employment is more than four weeks then it is likely that you will be entitled to the same amount of notice to leave your accommodation. For example, if you have been employed for six years, then by statute you are entitled to six weeks notice to terminate that employment, and therefore six weeks to leave your accommodation.

On the other hand, if you are entitled to less than four weeks notice under your contract of employment and, for example, your notice period is one week, then it is arguable that you are nevertheless entitled to more than one week's notice to leave the premises you occupy, if that is what is reasonable (again see below as to the requirement for a formal notice).

Is a formal notice necessary to end my licence?
This depends on whether you share the premises you occupy with your landlord or his family. If you do so share the premises there is no requirement that you are served with a formal notice.

If you do not share the premises with your landlord or his family then you are entitled to a written notice to quit which gives you at least four weeks notice that your licence will come to an end. This is so whether you are entitled to a shorter period of notice under your contract of employment, and whether twenty-eight days would be a longer period than was reasonable without this additional right. Also the notice must inform you that you need not leave your premises without a court order and that you should seek advice as to your rights. This information must be in the form prescribed by Parliament.

Does it make any difference if I am wrongfully or unfairly dismissed?
No. Your permission to stay in your flat is still withdrawn. If you were able to prove that your dismissal was unfair, at most you may be able to sue your landlord for damages, possibly to include damages for loss of your home.

Do I have to leave my accommodation as soon as my notice runs out?
If you have the right to decide who may or may not come

into your accommodation, known as the right to use the premises exclusively, then your landlord must go to court before he can require you actually to leave the premises. He will have to apply to the court for an order for possession. However, once he has proved that your permission to live in the accommodation has been withdrawn the court has no choice but to order you to leave. When the court makes an order against you, it does have the power to postpone for a limited period the date you must give up possession. It will do so if you can show that your personal circumstances justify a delay in your landlord's recovering his property.

If you do not have the right to use the premises exclusively then, strictly speaking, your landlord does not need to go to court in order to force you to leave. However, he would be well advised to do so and in most cases a landlord will take the precaution of bringing possession proceedings to establish his right to evict you. Again the court has no choice but to order possession in these proceedings and has only a limited power to postpone the date you must give up possession.

If you hope to obtain accommodation from your local authority after you have been evicted you would be well advised in either case to remain in your accommodation whenever possible, until an order for possession is made. This question is dealt with in more detail in Chapter 19 of this book.

5: Private Sector – Rents

Is there any control over how much rent a landlord may charge a tied occupier?
Yes. The level of control, however, varies depending on your status. The first distinction is between service tenants and service occupiers.

A. SERVICE OCCUPIERS

Service occupiers are a form of licensee and the position regarding your rent will in general be the same as for any other licensee in the private sector. Strictly speaking the money, if any, paid by a service occupier is not called 'rent', it is a 'licence fee', but for the sake of simplicity in this book it will be referred to as rent.

What rent do service occupiers have to pay?
The starting point for the amount of rent you should pay is the amount that was agreed between yourself and your landlord when you first started occupying your premises. In the case of service occupiers this may either be at the usual level you would expect for rented accommodation in the area or it may be a nominal amount which you pay from time to time or it may be an agreed amount which is deducted from your wages. Some service occupiers may pay no rent at all. If this is the case then it is likely that you are receiving a lower wage than you would if your accommodation was not provided with your job.

What should I be paying for in my rent?
This again will depend on what you agreed with your landlord. For a service occupier, rent can simply be the

fee you pay for the accommodation and you will be responsible for other outgoings; at the other extreme your rent might include contributions towards heating bills and food, etc. It is a good idea before you agree a rent on the latter basis to have a clear idea of what it is you are paying for and how much of the rent is going towards each bill, so that any necessary increase can be properly monitored.

Can my landlord increase my rent without my consent?
Strictly speaking no, unless it was part of the agreement between you when you first moved into the premises that the rent could be increased. If you appear to pay no rent but receive lower wages on account of the provision of accommodation, you may be subject to hidden increases such as a lower wage rise than you would expect at any particular time.

Can I do anything about my landlord trying to put up my rent?
Yes, in theory you would be entitled to require your landlord to abide by the agreement you made before moving into the premises. The main difficulty with this is that your bargaining power as a service occupier is diminished because of your limited security of tenure. When objecting to a rise in your rent you should bear in mind that your landlord has the final sanction of dismissal and the repossession of your home. It is likely that a dismissal on such grounds would not be fair but as mentioned on page 38 this would not necessarily prevent you losing your home. Negotiations regarding rent increases therefore should be handled diplomatically and also flexibly. If the increase is for a genuine reason, then probably too much objection should not be taken. It is best, if in any doubt, to obtain advice on your position.

What is the position if I get into arrears with my rent?
Failure to pay rent amounts to a breach of contract and, if he wished, your landlord could sue you for the debt. In addition your landlord may be prompted to take more drastic action against you, such as terminating your employment and seeking possession of your home. If you do get into arrears it is probably best to discuss this with your landlord and, if possible, to try to come to some arrangement for you to pay the arrears off, either in a lump sum or by instalments.

B. SERVICE TENANTS

The rules relating to rent are different depending on whether your tenancy began before or on or after 15 January 1989.

1. Tenancies Commencing Before 15 January 1989

What rent should I pay?
The amount of rent you should pay is initially whatever amount was agreed between you and your landlord when you first moved into your premises. This is known as the 'contractual rent'. The amount you agree can include other payments such as heating charges. If your rent also includes an amount attributable to meals or services then you may well be a licensee rather than a tenant (see Chapter 1).

Can my landlord put up my rent without my agreement?
Generally speaking no, unless at the time you made the agreement with your landlord it was part of that agreement that the rent could be increased. For example, you

may have been given a tenancy for three years and have agreed that the rent could be increased once a year on the anniversary of your taking the tenancy.

If you are not prepared to agree an increase in rent then the consequences are different depending on your status (see Chapter 1). There are rent controls set out in the Rent Act governing the position of regulated tenants, and to a lesser extent the position of restricted contract tenants. There are no controls in respect of those tenants who do not fit into either of these categories (i.e. you are excluded from protection), for example because you rent accommodation in on-licensed premises (see page 19). If you fall into this latter category then your landlord still may not increase the rent without your consent, but he can circumvent the need for your consent by terminating your tenancy (see Chapter 3, page 35) and granting you a new one at a higher rent. If you are neither a regulated nor a restricted contract tenant then you will have limited security of tenure. If you refuse to agree to an increase in rent this may prompt your landlord to take possession proceedings against you. In these circumstances it may be wiser to agree to a reasonable increase. If in any doubt you should take advice.

What are the rent controls for regulated tenants?

Rent controls for regulated tenants are based on a system of 'fair rents'. A 'fair rent' is one which has been fixed by a 'Rent Officer'. Either you or your landlord can apply to have a fair rent fixed. Application is made to your local Rent Office and forms can be obtained from the office itself. Often advice agencies keep forms and will help you to complete them.

What is a fair rent?

A fair rent is the amount fixed by the Rent Officer as being appropriate for the accommodation which you occupy. In deciding what is appropriate the Rent Officer takes into account the terms of your tenancy (for example whether you have use of a garden, etc.). He also takes into account the condition of the property, its size and type (for example whether it is self-contained, whether there are shared facilities, etc.) and its location (for example whether it is near to transport, shops, etc.). He does not take into account your personal circumstances.

The Rent Officer will also use 'comparables' to decide on a fair rent. This means that he will have regard to the levels of fair rents fixed for other properties of a similar type and in a similar location. You are entitled to inspect the register of fair rents and if you are contemplating applying for a fair rent it would be advisable to inspect the register to find out whether the rent you are already paying is higher or lower than fair rents in the vicinity of your home. If you have applied for a fair rent but are dissatisfied with the Rent Officer's decision then there is a right of appeal to the Rent Assessment Committee.

A fair rent is fixed in respect of your premises rather than in respect of your tenancy. Once a fair rent has been 'registered', i.e. finally decided and notified to you and your landlord, it is entered on to the register of fair rents. That then is the maximum rent that your landlord is entitled to charge for the premises, *whoever* is living there. Unless there is a material change in the premises (for example if they are completely refurbished or another room is added to the tenancy) a new fair rent cannot be applied for until two years have expired since the former registration.

What happens if the rent which is registered is less than my contractual rent?

In this case you should only pay the registered rent. Once a fair rent has been fixed, your landlord is not entitled to charge you any more.

What happens if the rent which is registered is more than my contractual rent?
In this case your landlord is not entitled to recover the new rent until he has done two things: first he must bring your contractual tenancy to an end (see page 20) and secondly he must serve you with a 'notice of increase'. This notice must be in a particular form laid down by Parliament. Your landlord can combine these two things by serving you with a notice of increase which also operates as a notice to quit (see page 21). In order to do this the notice of increase must not purport to increase your rent any time before your tenancy could have been brought to an end by a notice to quit. For example if you have a weekly tenancy then the notice of increase must give you four clear weeks notice of the date on which your rent will go up.

What if a fair rent had been fixed on my premises before I moved in?
In this case the registered rent is the maximum that your landlord is entitled to charge you. If your landlord has, unusually, been charging you less than the registered rent then the position is not affected. If your landlord wished to increase your rent he would still have to terminate your tenancy and serve you with a notice of increase.

If your landlord has been charging you more than the registered rent then you are entitled to recover any excess charged for the past two years. You can recover the excess either by taking your landlord to court or by withholding rent until the excess is balanced out. If you choose the latter course, it is better if you inform your landlord in writing of what you propose to do and calculate carefully how much you are entitled to withhold and when you will have to start paying rent again.

Can I recover excess rent which I have paid if my landlord has not terminated my tenancy or served me with a notice of increase prior to charging me a higher rent?
Yes, you can recover the excess paid in the same way as mentioned in the previous paragraph.

Can my landlord increase my rent without registration?
If no fair rent has been fixed then the maximum rent your landlord can charge is the contractual rent. If you are a contractual tenant (see pages 20–22) then your landlord can pass on to you any increases in services, if this was part of your original agreement.

There is an exception to the rule that the maximum rent which can be charged is the contractual rent unless and until registration. This is where you and your landlord enter into a 'rent agreement'. This is an agreement for you to pay a higher rent, and is invalid unless it is in writing, signed by you both and has a statement at the head of the document which, in summary, reminds you that your security of tenure will not be affected if you refuse to sign and that even if the agreement is signed you still have the right to have a fair rent registered.

What are the rent controls for restricted contract tenants?
Restricted contract tenants are not entitled to apply for the registration of fair rents. However there is an alternative system whereby restricted contract tenants may apply for a 'reasonable rent' to be determined and registered by the Rent Tribunal.

The system is similar to, but not the same as, that for the registration of fair rents. The registration of a reasonable rent applies to the property rather than the tenant and re-registration can be sought after two years. If after two years no restricted contract is in existence at the property the landlord can apply for the registration to be removed.

Any charge which exceeds an existing registration can be recovered for six years of excess. It is a criminal offence to overcharge a restricted contract tenant. This may be reported to the local authority's Tenancy Relations Officer, who may consider prosecution.

Before applying for the registration of a reasonable rent it is vital to remember that, as a restricted contract tenant, you have very limited security of tenure. If you seek to have your rent reduced you may spark retaliatory action from your landlord, who may then take possession proceedings against you.

If you have a tenancy which pre-dates 1980 and your landlord serves you with notice to quit in response to your application for a reasonable rent, this is automatically deferred until the hearing of the application and usually for six months afterwards. Your landlord has the right to apply for a reduction of this period. If your tenancy commenced after the 28 November 1980 then the tribunal does not have these powers with respect to your notice to quit (see page 23).

2. Tenancies Commencing After 15 January 1989

What rent should I pay?

The amount of rent you should pay is determined by what you have agreed with your landlord. This may include payments in respect of other charges such as gas and electricity. It is a good idea if you discover at the outset what proportion of your rent each charge represents.

Can my landlord increase my rent?
This depends on whether you are an assured tenant or are excluded from the protection given to assured tenants (see pages 30–31).

(a) If you are excluded from protection then, strictly speaking, your landlord cannot increase your rent without your consent. You may have agreed a formula for the increase of your rent when you moved into the premises, for example that the rent would go up by 15 per cent every year. If you have not agreed a formula and you do not agree to your rent being put up, your landlord has several choices. Either he can leave the rent at the same level or he can terminate your tenancy (see page 35) and grant you a new tenancy at a higher rent, or he can terminate your tenancy and obtain possession of the premises against you. Given that you have very little protection against eviction, you should consider your position very carefully before objecting to a rent rise. In particular you should weigh up whether the new rent your landlord is asking is unreasonably high and your prospects of obtaining alternative accommodation should your landlord decide to evict you. If possible in such a situation you should try and negotiate with your landlord for an increase which is not unreasonable.

(b) If you are an assured tenant then your landlord may seek to increase your rent without your consent in one of two ways:

(i) If it was part of the agreement for your tenancy that the rent could be varied, then your landlord may rely on that agreement and put your rent up accordingly.

(ii) If it was not part of your agreement that the rent could be varied then your landlord must follow a prescribed notice procedure. In summary this is as follows: your landlord may serve a notice on you proposing a new rent for your premises. The notice must be in a form prescribed by Parliament. Also it must specify the date on which he proposes that the new rent should take effect. That date must not be earlier than the first anniversary of your tenancy i.e. one year after it commenced and also it must not be earlier than the 'minimum period' after the date of the service of the notice. The 'minimum period' is different depending on what type of tenancy you have. If you have a yearly tenancy the minimum period is six months, if you have a monthly or weekly tenancy, the minimum period is a month, if you have any other type of periodic tenancy, the minimum period is the same as the period of your tenancy. For example, if you have a quarterly tenancy (three monthly) the minimum period will also be three months. The notice itself may be served at any time.

If the notice is valid and properly served then the new rent will take effect on the date specified in the notice *unless* you refer the notice to the Rent Assessment Committee. Alternatively, you can come to an agreement with your landlord that no rent increase is called for or a different rent increase is called for. If you wish to refer the notice to the Rent Assessment Committee you must do so before the 'minimum period' expires.

Once the notice has been referred to the Rent Assessment Committee they make a decision on what the increased rent should be. The rent fixed includes anything else which you initially agreed would be part of the rent such as a fixed heating charge.

After your rent has been raised in this way, your landlord may seek to increase the rent on each anniversary of the date your rent was first increased, and in the same way.

6: Private Sector – Sharing

Do tied occupiers have the right to share their premises?
Generally speaking yes, but whether you have the right to share the premises or not depends ultimately on what you have agreed with your landlord.

'Sharing' is not a legal term. Different labels are given to different sharing arrangements. The people you share with may be licensees or lodgers or may be 'subtenants'. You may wish to share your premises with your family, or you may wish to have a more formal arrangement to share your home with others who may be given their own room and pay you rent; alternatively you may wish to leave your premises for a time and allow another person to live in your premises during your absence.

What is the difference between a licensee or lodger and a subtenant?
In Chapter 1 the difference between a licensee and a tenant is explained. Those who share premises with you are your licensees, lodgers or tenants. Your tenants are known as subtenants because they are given a tenancy by you and not by your landlord.

As has been explained licensees have lesser rights of occupation than tenants; usually they will not have been given a room of their own. Even if they have been given a room of their own they may not be tenants if there is something in the arrangement between you that makes their right of occupation informal; the main examples of this are family arrangements and friends who come to stay on a temporary basis.

Lodgers will usually have rooms of their own but,

because you provide them with services such as cleaning, linen changes and meals, they are not tenants because you will require virtually unrestricted access to their room to carry out those services.

Subtenants have their own room or rooms and have the right to exclude anyone, including yourself, from that room.

If you leave your accommodation for a period, but let someone else use that accommodation in your absence, then they may either be a licensee or a subtenant. If you hand over your accommodation completely and give the person who is to occupy the premises the right to exclude anyone, including yourself, from the accommodation, they will be your subtenant. If the arrangement is more informal, and the person occupying is in effect a caretaker of the property on your behalf, then he will be a licensee.

Can I let someone in as my subtenant?

This depends on what the agreement between you and your landlord says. If the agreement makes no mention of subletting then you may sublet either all or part of the premises.

If your agreement does mention subletting then it will deal with the question in one of several ways; firstly the agreement may prohibit the subletting of all of the premises or part of the premises or both.

Secondly, the prohibition can take one of two forms. Either the prohibition can be absolute or qualified. An absolute prohibition is one which tells you that you are not allowed to sublet at all. A qualified prohibition is one which tells you that you are not allowed to sublet without first obtaining your landlord's consent. If your landlord's consent is required prior to subletting, then this consent must not be unreasonably withheld. What is reasonable or unreasonable depends on the facts of the particular case. If your landlord does refuse his consent for you to sublet, for no good reason (and it would be wise to take advice), then there are two alternative courses of action that you can take. Either you can apply to court for a declaration that your landlord's consent is being unreasonably withheld or go ahead and sublet taking the risk that retaliatory action may be taken against you.

Can I let someone in as my licensee or lodger?
Again this depends on what the agreement says. If it only forbids or restricts subletting, you have not broken a term of the agreement by taking in a lodger or licensee.

If I go away for a while, can I transfer my tenancy or licence to someone else during my absence?
If you let someone occupy your home whilst you are away temporarily then they will either be your subtenant or your licensee and you should see the answers to the previous questions as to whether this is permissible.

Can I transfer my tenancy or licence to someone else permanently?
Licences cannot be transferred to someone else, because they are personal rights of occupation.

Whether a tenancy can be transferred depends firstly on what the agreement between you and your landlord says. Agreements often prohibit permanent transfers known as assignments or prohibit them without first obtaining your landlord's consent. (This is the same provision as for subletting, see above).

A statutory tenancy (see page 22) cannot be assigned but it can be transferred. To transfer a statutory tenancy it is necessary to have a written agreement to which you, your landlord and the person who is going to take over the premises are parties.

To carry out an assignment, it is necessary that it

is in writing and signed by the parties. If the assignment is not in writing and signed then it may be effective against you, but it will not be effective against your landlord unless and until he treats the new occupier as a tenant, for example by accepting rent in the knowledge that the new person has taken over from you.

Can my family take over my tenancy or licence?

A transfer between members of the family is an assignment like any other. If you die, the position is different. Licences cannot be inherited. If you are a sole tenant then on your death the tenancy passes to your next of kin, or if you have made a will, to whosoever you have left it to.

There are however special rules affecting the tenancies of regulated (see page 23) and assured tenants (see page 30). In both cases the inheritance of tenancies is governed by special provision which override the usual inheritance rules.

1. Regulated Tenants

If the deceased tenant was married then his spouse (or common law spouse, i.e. man and woman living together as husband and wife) will succeed to the tenancy, as a statutory tenant (see page 22).

If the deceased tenant has no spouse, then any member of the family living with the tenant at the time of his death and for two years beforehand is entitled to succeed to the tenancy, but the tenancy will be an assured tenancy (see page 30).

There is one exception to this rule and that is where the tenant dies at any time between 15 January 1989 and the 15 July 1990; then a member of the family may succeed to the tenancy as an assured tenant if they resided with the deceased tenant for six months prior to 15 January 1989.

'Living with' means living with as a home, not merely visiting occasionally.

On the death of a 'successor spouse' a member of the family (of both the original tenant and the successor) who has lived with the 'successor spouse' for two years prior to their death is entitled to succeed to the tenancy.

If there is a dispute as to who should take over the tenancy, then the possible successors can apply to the court for a decision.

2. Assured Tenants

If the deceased tenant was married, then his spouse (or common law spouse) will succeed to the tenancy as an assured tenant, provided that immediately before his death she was occupying the premises as her only or principal home. There can be no succession by a spouse if the tenant was himself a successor.

There is no provision for any succession by members of the deceased tenant's family, other than his spouse.

7: Tenancies in the Public Sector

What is the public sector?

The public sector is the description given to accommodation owned and rented by 'public sector landlords'. Probably the largest providers of 'public sector' housing are local authorities. For the purposes of this book two other sets of organizations should be noted as providing public sector accommodation:

Housing associations or trusts: housing associations and trusts are organizations which provide housing, usually with the assistance of public funds. In order to obtain these funds the organizations must 'register' with a central body known as the Housing Corporation. If you live in accommodation provided by a registered housing association or trust you are treated as being in the public sector, and this section of the book applies to you. However, this is so only if your tenancy commenced before 15 January 1989. If your tenancy commenced on or after that date, then you are treated in the same way as assured tenants in the private sector (see Chapter 3, pages 30–34). If your housing association is not registered, then you fall within the private sector and should see Chapters 2–6.

Development corporations: These are organizations which have been appointed instead of local authorities to manage housing in specified areas, for example new towns are managed by appointed boards. Development corporations include the Development Board for Rural Wales and urban development corporations. If you rent premises from any of these you fall within the public sector.

Recently the government has made provision for large-scale sale of local authority housing stock. If you are in an area where this has occurred you will only continue to be within the public sector if the ownership of the property has passed to a Housing Action Trust. Once the ownership of your property has passed to a private landlord you will become an assured tenant in the private sector (see pages 30–34).

The 'public sector' does not include property owned and rented by the Crown or Government Departments. In the case of Crown property, if this is under the management of an agency known as the Crown Estates Commissioners then you will be a private sector tenant and either a regulated or assured tenant (Chapter 3); otherwise Crown tenants and government department tenants are wholly without protection.

Other bodies which may sound public, such as the Church Commissioners, the British Museum or nationalized industries, are treated in the same way as private landlords and you should see Chapters 2–6 of this book for your rights.

Do all those who live in the public sector have the same rights?

No. Most of those who live in the public sector are secure tenants; additionally some occupiers are known as secure licensees. For most purposes, the distinction between tenants and licensees is not important in the public sector; in particular their rights of security of tenure are the same.

As far as tied occupiers are concerned you may fall into a separate category who will be referred to in this book as 'residential occupiers'. Residential occupiers have far less security than others living in the public sector. There is also a residual category of secure tenants who are vulnerable to additional ground for possession who will be referred to as secure service tenants (see pages 59 and 63–65).

What is a secure tenant?

A secure tenant is one renting accommodation from one of the above mentioned landlords. The rights of secure tenants are mainly embodied in the Housing Act 1985. That Act provides that there are certain exceptions to being a secure tenant. The main exceptions are:

(a) tenancies for more than twenty-one years;

(b) temporary accommodation provided during the course of works to your home;

(c) student lettings;

(d) temporary accommodation provided to you as a homeless person (see Chapter 19). This exception applies if you have been provided with accommodation whilst inquiries are made about your case, or you have been found to be intentionally homeless, or you are being housed whilst waiting to be re-housed by another local authority. In all these cases you will not have a secure tenancy for a period of twelve months, starting from the date they tell you what their decision is. If, at the end of that twelve months your right to live in your premises has not been terminated, you then become a secure tenant;

(e) tenancies of dwellings situated in on-licenced premises (not off-licences);

(f) temporary accommodation for persons taking up employment. The last exception applies if you move to a new area and need temporary accommodation. If you are housed in public sector accommodation you will not be a secure tenant if:

(i) you are given the accommodation in order to take up your employment *and*

(ii) you were notified in writing that the exception would apply to you.

This exemption only applies for the first year you are in occupation of the premises. Therefore if you lawfully stay in the accommodation for more than a year, you will become a secure tenant.

Additionally in all cases of public sector housing you are only a secure tenant for so long as you live in your premises as your 'only or principal home'. Therefore, if you permanently move away from your premises you will no longer be secure. On the other hand a temporary absence will not deprive you of security.

Am I a residential occupier?

You are a residential occupier and consequently not a secure tenant if the following three conditions apply to you:

(a) you live in accommodation provided by a public body *and*

(b) your landlord is also your employer or is a local authority, a development corporation, or a Housing Action Trust *and*

(c) your contract of employment requires you to occupy your accommodation for the better performance of your duties.

This latter requirement is similar to the requirement set out on page 15 in relation to service occupiers in the private sector. It means that you occupy your accommodation because your employer requires you to do so, and it is necessary for you to do so in order to carry out your job properly. Necessary in this context does not mean merely more convenient; there must be a true connection between the nature of your work and the requirement for you to live on the premises. For example, in some cases a caretaker of a block of flats who must be on 24-hour call would have to live in or very near the block in order to carry out his duties.

Just because you are employed by a public body and live in accommodation provided by your employer does not mean that you are not a secure tenant. It may simply be a coincidence and in an area where a local authority has a great deal of housing stock and employ a large number of people it is a common situation. If it is merely a coincidence that your landlord is your employer, and if there is no connection between your employment and your accommodation, then you will be a secure tenant and *not* just a residential occupier. Even if there is some connection between your employment and your accommodation but the connection is *not* one which makes it necessary for you to live in a certain property in order to carry out your job properly, then you will be a secure tenant.

There are additionally two specific categories of residential occupiers, they are:

(d) police officers who live in public sector accommodation which is provided for them, by a public sector landlord (see page 55) free of rent, and

(e) firemen whose duties require them to live in close proximity to a particular fire station *and* the accommodation was let to them, by a public sector landlord, because of that requirement.

Am I a secure service tenant?

If your accommodation was granted to you as a consequence of your employment and your home is part of or in the grounds of a building which is not 'mainly used' for housing then you are a secure service tenant.

The condition that your home is granted to you 'as a consequence' of your employment is not the same as it being 'necessary' for you to live in particular premises to carry out your work. The connection between your job and your home therefore does not have to be as close as the connection which would render you a residential occupier. What is necessary however is to show that if it had not been for your employment you would not have been provided with your accommodation.

There are not many secure service tenants because the accommodation at which the limitation of security is aimed is not part of the normal housing stock.

Do I have a secure tenancy if I am let premises which have been used as 'tied accommodation' for residential occupiers in the past?

The fact that premises have been used by residential occupiers in the past, in some cases temporarily, prevents an occupier, who would otherwise be a secure tenant, from having full security of tenure.

In order for this specific exemption to apply the following conditions must have been met:

(a) the premises you live in must have been used at some time in the three years before you were allowed to live there as accommodation for a residential occupier, and

(b) before your tenancy began, you must have been notified in writing of the fact that the premises had been used for a residential occupier and that you would not be a secure tenant until you had occupied the premises for three years.

For example, you may be given a flat which, until you moved in, had been a caretaker's flat. If the offer of the flat has nothing to do with work, but you are notified before you take the tenancy that you will not be a secure tenant for three years because of the previous letting, you will fall within this exception. If after three years your right to live there has not been terminated (see page 66) you will then become a secure tenant of the premises.

8: Secure Tenants and Secure Licensees – Security of Tenure

Do all secure tenants and licensees (see page 56) have the same security of tenure?
Generally speaking yes. In this chapter all references to secure tenancies are applicable to secure licences.

How can my landlord force me to leave my accommodation?
Your landlord can only force you to leave your accommodation when he has obtained an order for possession against you from the court. This is true of all secure tenants, including the residual category of secure service tenants (see page 59). To obtain such an order he must first serve a 'notice seeking possession' on you, and then prove that there is a 'ground' for possession against you.

What is a 'notice seeking possession'?
This is a written notice in a specific form which warns you that your landlord is contemplating taking possession proceedings. The notice will tell you what ground or grounds your landlord will rely on to try and obtain the order and will state that the proceedings will not commence before a specified date. The notice seeking possession is only in force for one year from the earliest date the landlord can start the court proceedings.

If you receive a notice seeking possession you should not ignore it. In particular if the notice alleges some default such as arrears of rent or breach of a term of tenancy, or nuisance which you can rectify, you should do so. Otherwise take advice at the earliest opportunity.

What are the 'grounds' for possession?

These are the reasons for which the court can order you to leave your home. There are three types of grounds available against secure tenants:

(a) Discretionary grounds – to obtain an order for possession on the basis of one of these grounds the court has to be satisfied, in addition to the ground being made out, that it is reasonable to evict. The test of reasonableness is the same as for private tenants (see page 24). The discretionary grounds are: rent arrears, breach of another term of the tenancy, nuisance and annoyance, damage to the premises or furniture, the obtaining of the tenancy by knowingly or recklessly giving a false statement, the payment of a premium for an exchange and, lastly, that the tenant is in occupation of premises which were only made available whilst works were carried out at another dwelling where he was a secure tenant. There is a further ground against secure service tenants which is dealt with below.

(b) Grounds where suitable alternative accommodation is available – here the court need not consider reasonableness but must be satisfied that the tenant will be provided with suitable alternative accommodation. This is defined in similar terms as suitable alternative accommodation in the private sector (see page 26).

The grounds are: that the tenant's home is statutorily overcrowded, that the landlord wishes to demolish or reconstruct the building the accommodation is in, and cannot do so without first obtaining possession, that the dwelling is in an area of redevelopment for which possession is required, that the landlord is a charity and the tenant's continued occupation of the dwelling would conflict with the object of the charity.

(c) Grounds where both suitable alternative accommodation is available and the court is satisfied that it is reasonable to order possession. (For reasonableness see page 24). One of these grounds relates to special housing which is being occupied by tenants who do not themselves require special housing; another ground is available against a tenant who is occupying housing which is more extensive than is reasonably required by him, i.e. the premises have more rooms than are needed by the tenant *and* the tenant has inherited the premises (see page 73) and was not the spouse of the deceased tenant.

There are two further grounds available against secure service tenants (see below).

What are the additional grounds available against me if I am a secure service tenant?

There are two extra grounds for possession available against you over and above those usually available against secure tenants. Both grounds are discretionary and require the court to be satisfied on reasonableness (see page 24). The second ground for possession as well as being discretionary also requires your landlord to prove that suitable alternative accommodation (see page 26) will be available if an order for possession is made. The grounds are:

(a) That your accommodation is part of, or in the grounds of a building which is used mainly for purposes other than housing *and* that you were granted a tenancy of your accommodation as a consequence of your employment by your landlord or a local authority, a development corporation or the governors of an aided school. Also that you or anyone residing with you has behaved in such a way that, having regard to the use of the building your accommodation is part of, it would not be right for you to continue to live there.

This ground envisages that you or someone residing with you has been guilty of misconduct of some kind. The particular type of misconduct must relate to the use of the building in which your accommodation is situated. The misconduct could be of any type – for example, noise, or damage to property either to the premises rented or to the building the accommodation is situate in. This ground only applies to you if you were granted a tenancy of your accommodation as a consequence of your employment; it probably does not matter that you did not know that was the reason you were let the premises, and it also appears that it is not relevant that you may have left that employment since you first moved in.

Since this is a discretionary ground, once the facts of the case have been established the court would have then to be satisfied that it is reasonable to make an order for possession against you. This involves taking into account all your personal circumstances such as your age, income, the reason for your behaviour, your family circumstances; and also taking into account the circumstances of your landlord.

(b) The second ground is that your accommodation is part of, or in the grounds of, a building which is used mainly for purposes other than housing or is a cemetery *and* that you were granted a tenancy of your accommodation as a consequence of your employment by your landlord or a local authority or a development corporation or the governors of an aided school *and* that your employment has ceased *and* that your landlord reasonably requires your accommodation for another employee *and* that there will be suitable alternative accommodation available for you.

This ground envisages no misconduct on your part, merely that your employment has ceased and that your landlord requires the accommodation for another employee. Your landlord must 'reasonably require' the premises, this is in addition to the general question of reasonableness. The accommodation which you are offered to replace your own has to be of similar security, and could either be another secure tenancy or accommodation in the private sector let under a protected or assured tenancy. It must also be reasonably suitable to your needs, which include your family's needs. For example, it would have to be sufficiently accessible to your work, your wife's work and your children's schools and it would have to be big enough for you and your family.

If the court made an order for possession against me, when would I have to leave the property?

This depends on the discretion of the judge who has power to postpone an order for possession for whatever period he feels is reasonable.

The judge also has the power to 'suspend' an order for possession in cases where 'reasonableness' must be considered. This means that although he makes an order for possession it would not take effect at all if you complied with any conditions he made as a basis for you to stay. After a specified period, the possession order should cease to be effective. For example, if your landlord sought a possession order against you on the basis of your conduct in that you were too noisy, the judge could make an order for possession but suspend it on the basis that you ceased to make excessive noise, and that after two years the order was to have no effect.

9: Residential Occupiers – Security of Tenure

Do all residential occupiers (see page 58) have the same security of tenure?
No. There are some variations dependent on whether you are a tenant or a licensee and whether you have the power to exclude others from your accommodation or not. If you are entitled to decide who shall or shall not come into your accommodation, then you will have greater protection than otherwise. For all residential occupiers, however, security of tenure is limited. All your landlord needs to do is to terminate your right to occupy your premises and then, in most cases to apply to the court for an order for possession which the court has no power to refuse.

How can my landlord terminate my right to occupy my premises?
This depends on whether you are a tenant or a licensee. If you are a tenant then your right to occupy your premises is terminated in the same way as tenancies in the private sector, (see page 35). Once your tenancy has been terminated however you do not become a 'statutory tenant', your tenancy does not continue and your landlord need only apply to the court stating that he requires possession of the premises. He need not prove any 'grounds' for possession.

If you are a licensee then your right to occupy your premises is terminated in the same way as for service occupiers in the private sector, see pages 36–39.

Does my landlord have to go to court in order to evict me?

Your landlord has to go to court to obtain an order for possession against you if you are a tenant or if you are a licensee who is entitled to exclude others from your accommodation. If you are a licensee who is not so entitled then strictly speaking your landlord does not need to go to court but would be well advised to do so. Once your landlord has properly terminated your right to occupy your premises and has made an application to court for possession, the judge has no choice but to order you to leave; however he does have power to delay the date the order is to take effect for a few weeks. If you wish to seek local authority accommodation after you have been evicted you would be well advised to stay in your accommodation until an order for possession is made against you. This is so even if you are aware that you would not be able successfully to defend the proceedings (see Chapter 19).

Does it make a difference if I was unfairly or wrongfully dismissed?

No, your permission to occupy your premises has still been withdrawn and your landlord would be entitled to go on and obtain an order for possession against you.

If your landlord has acted quite outrageously in dismissing you, or in deciding to take possession proceedings against you, then you may in an exceptional case be able to challenge the possession proceedings on that basis. Unfortunately a successful argument on this basis would be extremely rare.

10: Public Sector – Rents

What rent do I have to pay to my landlord?
The starting point is what is in the agreement with your landlord. Your rent may include other charges such as heating. The position in regard to rent is different depending on whether your landlord is a housing association or one of the other public bodies described in Chapter 7.

A. LOCAL AUTHORITIES/ DEVELOPMENT CORPORATIONS AND HOUSING ACTION TRUSTS

How is the level of rent decided?
These authorities have a legal duty to charge a 'reasonable' rent, but it is for them to decide what is reasonable. This can vary from something close to what the premises cost to provide, to a low rent subsidized from public funds.

Local authorities receive public subsidies for their housing functions. What they receive depends in part on their rental income. However, the Government provides subsidy not on what rental income the authority actually receives, but on what the Government thinks they ought to receive.

How can my landlord increase the rent?
This depends on whether or not you are a secure tenant.

1. Secure Tenants
Unless your agreement with your landlord contains a provision enabling your landlord to increase your rent, it

can only be changed by notice of variation. This is a document which is served on you and tells you that on a date in the future the rent will change. If you have a weekly tenancy you are entitled to four weeks' notice. If you have any other type of periodic tenancy, for example monthly or yearly, then you are entitled to notice which is equivalent to the length of that period.

2. Non-secure Tenants

The position is different depending on whether you are a tenant or a licensee.

If you are a tenant then your landlord has a choice. Firstly, the agreement may provide for increase; secondly, you may agree the change; thirdly, there is a notice of variation procedure similar to that applicable to secure tenants and, finally, your landlord can serve a notice to quit (see pages 21–22) and grant a new tenancy at a higher rent.

If you are a licensee, your landlord has less choice. If the agreement between you does not allow for an increase, and if you do not agree the change in rent then your landlord can only increase the rent by terminating your licence (see pages 36–39) and granting you a new licence.

If you are a non-secure occupier you may wish to agree to the increase in rent if invited to do so, rather than take the risk that your right to occupy will not be renewed following termination as described above.

Can I challenge a rent increase by my landlord?

In theory, yes – for example, on the basis that what is being charged is unreasonably high. In practice this is extremely unlikely to succeed, and you would certainly need advice and assistance.

B. HOUSING ASSOCIATIONS

How are housing association rents decided?
This depends on whether you are a licensee or a tenant (see pages 9–12).

1. Licensees
Rents for licences are decided by the landlord and generally speaking there can be no challenge.

2. Tenants
This depends on whether your tenancy commenced before or on or after 15 January 1989:

(a) Pre-15 January 1989 – your rent is governed by the system of rent registration described in Chapter 5 on page 43. If a fair rent was not registered when you moved into the premises then you can apply for this to be done. However it is extremely unlikely that this has occurred. Any rent increase is determined within the system of rent registration, by application to the Rent Officer.

(b) Post-15 January 1989 – since you are an assured tenant, your rent is determined initially by your landlord, thereafter increases will occur in the same way as for other assured tenants (see Chapter 5, pages 48–49).

11: Public Sector – Sharing

Am I allowed to share my home?
If you are a secure tenant, normally yes. You can share with any member of your family. In addition you have a right to take in lodgers and subtenants, although in the latter case only with the consent of your landlord.

The rights of non-secure occupiers, including residential occupiers, are much fewer than those of secure tenants.

In the course of this chapter, words such as subtenant, licensee and lodger are used, see Chapter 1, pages 9–12 and Chapter 6, pages 50–52 for explanations of these terms.

A. SECURE TENANTS

Can I allow lodgers and licensees to live in my home?
Yes, you may allow anyone you like to live as a lodger in your property.

Can I sublet my home?
You can sublet part of your premises with the consent of your landlord. You cannot sublet the whole of the premises.

How do I get consent to a subletting of part?
Ask for it, preferably in writing, and keep a copy of the letter. Your landlord can only refuse to consent to a subletting of part if it is reasonable to do so. For example, it may be reasonable to refuse consent if the subletting would lead to overcrowding.

If your landlord refuses consent, he is obliged to give you a written statement of the reasons for his refusal. Also the consent cannot be given subject to a condition. For example, only on payment of your own arrears of rent.

If your landlord does not answer your request for consent, the law treats the landlord as having refused consent.

What do I do if the landlord refuses consent?

If your landlord refuses consent and you consider the refusal to be unreasonable, there are two courses of action open to you: either you can go to court to ask for a declaration that consent has been unreasonably withheld or you could go ahead with the subletting and take the risk that your landlord might take possession proceedings against you for breach of a term of your tenancy. In the latter case you could defend the proceedings on the basis that the refusal was unreasonable.

Going ahead with the subletting and waiting for your landlord to act is, of course, much more risky than making an application to court.

Can I sublet the whole of my premises, even for a short time?

No. This will be in breach of a term of your tenancy, and you may well be regarded as having given up occupation of the premises as an only or main home (see pages 57–58) so that you have ceased to be a secure tenant.

Can I hand over my tenancy to someone else?

With certain important exceptions, no. The exceptions relate to what happens on your death and handing over (assignment) to members of your family.

1. Transfer on death

When a secure tenant dies his secure tenancy may pass to a successor. This can only occur once, therefore it is not possible to acquire a tenancy on the death of a successor.

If the secure tenant was married, then his spouse will succeed to the tenancy provided she was living in the premises as her only or main home at the time of the tenant's death. If the tenant was not married, then the tenancy will pass to any member of the tenant's family who was living with the tenant at the time of his death and for a year beforehand.

2. Transfers to members of the family

As stated above the general rule is that a secure tenancy cannot be transferred (assigned). However a secure tenancy is capable of being assigned to a person who could have succeeded to the tenancy in the event of the tenant's death, as long as the tenancy agreement with the landlord does not prevent this.

The agreement with your landlord might say nothing about assignment. If this is so then you may assign your tenancy to any one of the people who could have succeeded you on your death i.e. your wife or a member of your family who has been residing with you for one year prior to the assignment. If you wish to assign your tenancy, this must be done by a 'deed', which is a sealed document preferably drawn up by a solicitor.

On the other hand your agreement with your landlord may either forbid any assignment (known as an absolute prohibition), or forbid assignment without your landlord's consent (known as a qualified prohibition).

(a) Absolute prohibitions: if your agreement prohibits assignment then strictly speaking that is the end of the matter. However, if you still go ahead with the assignment to a permitted person the tenancy continues, but there is a breach of the terms of the tenancy and hence a ground for possession proceedings to be brought against you (see page 62). In those proceedings you may be able to argue that notwithstanding the breach it would not be reasonable to make an order for possession against you (see pages 24–62).

(b) Qualified prohibitions: where your agreement prohibits assignment without your landlord's consent, then that consent cannot be unreasonably withheld. This is the same position as for private tenants and see page 51 for what this means.

B. NON-SECURE OCCUPIERS

Can I share my home?

This depends on what your agreement with your landlord says. If the agreement doesn't deal with sharing or subletting then you are free to share and sublet as you wish, always bearing in mind your limited security of tenure.

If the agreement prohibits sharing or subletting, then that is the end of the matter and to do so would be in breach of the agreement.

If the agreement prohibits sharing or subletting without your landlord's consent then the position is different depending on whether you are a licensee or a tenant. If you are a licensee then that permission may be withheld for any reason. If you are a tenant then the permission cannot be unreasonably withheld (see page 52 for what this means).

Can I hand over my right to occupy to someone else?

This depends on whether you have a licence or a tenancy. If you have a licence then you cannot hand this over, since all you have is a personal right of occupation.

If you have a tenancy then the question is decided on the basis of the agreement between you and your landlord. As with subletting the agreement may be silent on the question or contain an absolute or qualified prohibition. See page 51 for what this means.

12: Public Sector – Right to Buy

As a tied occupier, do I have the right to buy my home?

In the public sector you have the right to buy your home if you are a secure tenant and fulfil the residence condition described below. The right is not given to residential occupiers (see page 58) or to the category of occupiers described in this book as secure service tenants (see page 59). Even if you are a secure tenant there are certain exemptions to the right to buy which are set out below. Some of the important questions regarding right to buy are dealt with in this chapter, for more detail you should see *The Private Tenants Handbook*.

If you do not have the right to buy your home, your landlord may agree to sell it to you on a voluntary basis.

If you used to be a secure tenant but have become an assured tenant on a change of landlord (see pages 55–56), you may still have something called 'the preserved right to buy'. If you fall into this category you should see *The Private Tenants Handbook* for your rights.

Are both houses and flats for sale?

Yes. You will be entitled to either a freehold (i.e. outright ownership) or long lease of a house, or a long lease of a flat.

What conditions need to be fulfilled before I may exercise my right to buy?

The condition is that you must have been a public tenant for two years. This is not the same as having been a secure tenant with your present landlord. Any period as a secure tenant will qualify, regardless of whether or not with your present landlord, and regardless of whether this is a continuous period as a secure tenant or several periods broken up by periods when you were not a secure tenant.

You cannot rely, however, on periods of time when your landlord was a housing association which was either a charity or a housing association which has never received public funds (see below for general exemptions).

In some cases you can rely on someone else's period of occupation as a public tenant as well. You can add the periods your spouse – or a deceased spouse – has spent as a public sector tenant, or as the spouse of a public sector tenant. This is so only if they were periods when you and your spouse were living together, and if the spouse whose periods of time you want to add has died, if you were living together at the time of death.

Also if you succeeded to the tenancy (see page 73) or took it over by way of family transfer (see page 73), you can add the period you lived in the property before you took over the tenancy, provided that:

(a) it is a period since you turned 16, and

(b) there was no more than a two-year break in the period you want to claim.

What are the exemptions to the right to buy?

The exemptions are:

(a) The landlord is a housing association which is a charity, or which has at no time received public funds for its work.

(b) A court order has been made against you, which requires you to give up occupation at a specific date (see Chapter 8).

(c) There is a bankruptcy petition pending against you, or your joint tenant, or an order or arrangements have been made relating to bankruptcy.

(d) Your premises are part of, or are within the

grounds of, a non-housing building (for example a school), or a cemetery, and the tenancy was granted in connection with a job. This is the exemption which applies to secure service tenants, see page 59.

(e) The premises are designed for occupation by the physically disabled and they are part of a group of premises let out for occupation by the physically disabled and special support facilities are provided nearby.

(f) The premises are part of a group of properties let for occupation by those who are suffering or have suffered from mental disorders and facilities are provided nearby for their benefit.

(g) The premises are part of a group of properties suitable for occupation by the elderly, are normally let to the elderly and facilities are provided nearby for their benefit.

(h) The property is particularly suitable for an elderly person, and was let for occupation by either an elderly person or a physically handicapped person.

(i) The landlord does not own the freehold or have a lease with more than 21 years left to run.

(j) When the full procedure for right to buy has been completed, the landlord may refuse to sell if you are four or more weeks in arrears with rent or other payment. (See Chapter 10 for rents generally).

What will I have to pay?

You have to pay the market value of the property less a discount. The market value is calculated as at the date of your claim to buy, so that subsequent delays will not cause a price rise.

The discount you will be entitled to is based on the qualifying years of residence described above. In the case of a house you will get 32 per cent off the market price for two years' qualifying time, plus one per cent for each additional full year, to a maximum of 60 per cent. In the case of a flat, the figures are 44 per cent, plus 2 per cent per year, to a maximum of 70 per cent.

Are there any circumstances where I would have to pay back the discount?
Yes. If you dispose of the property, otherwise than by a family transaction within three years of buying, you have to repay the whole of the discount, less one third for each full year of occupation since purchase. Family transaction includes transfer on death or divorce. For other cases you should take advice.

How do I exercise the right to buy?
All the public-sector landlords whose secure tenants have the right to buy have forms on which you can apply. They must supply you with one within seven days of a request.

Once you have sent your form to your landlord, they must reply within a period of four to eight weeks admitting or denying your right to buy. Your claim may be denied on the basis of the exemptions set out above.

If you disagree with your landlord's denial of your right to buy you should take advice on how to challenge it.

Within a further eight weeks in the case of a freehold, or twelve weeks in the case of a lease, the landlord should write to you setting out its view of price, terms, discount, etc. Your landlord will also advise you of the right to refer the price to the District Valuer, and the right to claim a mortgage, and provide a form with which to do so.

You would be well advised to seek legal help on the completion of all these forms.

Can I back out of right to buy?
Yes. At any time before the transaction is completed you can withdraw your claim. You can, if you like, restart as soon as you want to do so, though of course at risk of a higher price.

13: What is an Agricultural Worker?

What is an agricultural worker?
For the purposes of this book you are an agricultural worker if you work in agriculture (see further below) and are provided with accommodation in connection with that work by your employer.

Do all agricultural workers have the same rights?
No. As an agricultural occupier you may qualify for similar protection afforded to other private sector tenants and be a regulated or assured tenant (see pages 18 and 30) or you may be one of a large number of agricultural workers who are given special rights and are known as protected agricultural occupiers.

Special rights are conferred on agricultural workers because many pay a very low rent or no rent at all and also many have licence agreements as opposed to tenancy agreements and for one or both reasons do not qualify as regulated tenants.

In order to qualify for these special rights certain conditions have to be met. We will examine those conditions in this chapter.

If you are not a regulated or assured tenant and do not fulfil the conditions set out below this does not mean you have no rights at all. You may instead be an agricultural service licensee and have some greater rights than other service licensees in the private sector.

Do I qualify for the rights given to other private sector tenants?
If you have a tenancy of premises let as a dwelling house

and pay rent, yes (see Chapter 2, page 13). If the reason that you do not qualify for those rights is that you pay a low rent or no rent or that you have a licence rather than a tenancy, then you may instead be entitled to the special rights given to protected agricultural occupiers.

Am I a protected agricultural occupier?

You are a protected agricultural occupier if you fulfil four conditions which relate: firstly, to the type of agreement you have with your landlord for your accommodation; secondly to who your landlord is or in legal terms whether your accommodation is in 'qualifying ownership'; thirdly what type of work you do and, fourthly, whether you work enough hours and have worked for enough time in agriculture to be known as a 'qualifying worker'.

These conditions are explained in greater detail below.

What sort of agreement is necessary in regard to my accommodation?

You must have a licence or a tenancy of residential accommodation which gives you the right to exclude from the premises all other people including your landlord. This is similar to the rights of occupation necessary to have a regulated or assured tenancy. But in order to qualify for the rights given to protected agricultural occupiers you may have either a tenancy *or* a licence, as long as you have the right to exclude anyone you wish from your premises. Furthermore it makes no difference if you pay no rent or only a very low rent.

If there is any other reason why you would not have the full protection afforded to private sector tenants, you will not qualify for the special protection given to agricultural occupiers. For example, if your landlord lives on the premises, you will not qualify for special protection.

Also there is a special exclusion which applies to agricultural workers in hostels. It is that if you only have one room to yourself with shared use of other rooms such as the kitchen and bathroom with other tenants, in premises where at least three other rooms are let or are available for letting on the same basis, then you will not qualify for the special rights.

Does my landlord have to fit into any special category?

Your landlord must have a connection with your work. He can either by your employer as well as being your landlord or he can be a person with whom your employer has made arrangements for your accommodation to be used as housing.

The connection with your work does not have to last throughout the whole time you occupy the premises. If there has been a connection at any time during your occupation then the condition is fulfilled. This condition is known as 'qualifying ownership'.

What is meant by 'agriculture' for the purposes of obtaining special rights?

The term 'agriculture' has a very wide definition, the list includes:

(a) Dairy farming and livestock keeping and breeding. Livestock includes any animal which is kept for the production of food, wool, skins or fur or the purposes of its use in carrying on any agricultural activity. Animal includes bird but not fish. The definition therefore includes intensive stock farming or factory farming;

(b) the production of any consumable produce which is grown for sale or consumption or other use for the purposes of trade or business or any other undertaking. This includes, for example, the growing of crops by hydroponics or in plastic bags;

(c) the use of land as grazing, meadow or pasture land or orchard or osier land;

(d) the use of land for market gardens or nursery grounds;

(e) forestry which includes the use of land for woodlands where that use is ancillary to the use of land for other agricultural purposes.

If your work fits within this list then you work in agriculture for the purpose of obtaining special rights. However, although the list is wide not every activity is included in the definition; for example, in one case a gamekeeper whose job it was to keep and rear pheasants was held not to be within the category of working in agriculture since the pheasants were kept primarily for sport.

Am I a qualifying worker?

You are a qualifying worker if *either*:

(a) you work whole time in agriculture *and* you have done this work for at least 91 weeks out of the previous 104 weeks. The number of weeks you have worked is calculated as at the time you wish to enforce your rights; or

(b) you are a permit worker and have worked as such for at least 91 out of the previous 104 weeks.

What counts as working 'whole time'?

'Whole time' means 35 hours per week of work in agriculture or working on activities connected or incidental to your work in agriculture. For example, if you only do casual work which does not require you to work 35 hours per week you would not be entitled to special rights.

Whole-time work in agriculture includes an apprenticeship in agriculture. Also, if your employer has agreed that you may have time off during any particular week or if you are on a holiday to which you are entitled or if you are off sick, then you will still be counted as having worked a full week of whole-time work. This is so both for the purposes of calculating your hours of work and for calculating whether or not you have worked 91 weeks out of 104.

What if I am prevented from working for a prolonged period or permanently as a result of an injury or disease suffered as a result of my work in agriculture?

If you suffered an injury disabling you and preventing you from working or if you have contracted a disease which can be shown to be caused by your work and at the time you were injured or caught the disease you were working whole time in agriculture or were a permit worker then you may have a 'qualifying injury or disease'.

If you have a qualifying injury or disease then notwithstanding that you are unable to work, the period during which you are so disabled will count towards the qualifying period of 91 weeks out of the previous 104.

Does it make any difference if I agree to move to new accommodation or sign a new agreement for my accommodation?

No, as long as you fulfilled the four conditions set out above immediately before you moved or signed the new agreement.

What rights do I have if I do *not* fulfil all of the special conditions?

This will depend on your individual situation, and the considerations in relation to the status of occupiers in the private sector generally will be applicable to you, see pages 13–17.

14: Protected Agricultural Occupiers – Security of Tenure

Do all protected agricultural occupiers have the same security of tenure?

No. The term protected agricultural occupier as used in this chapter refers to the special category of occupiers described in the last chapter. If you qualify for these rights then your security differs depending on whether your right to occupy your premises commenced before or after 15 January 1989. If your right to occupy your premises commenced before 15 January 1989 you have a 'protected occupancy'. If your rights commenced after that date you have an 'assured agricultural occupancy'. We will deal with these categories separately.

A. RIGHTS OF OCCUPATION COMMENCING BEFORE 15 JANUARY 1989 – PROTECTED OCCUPANCIES

Can my landlord force me to leave my home?

Your landlord can only force you to leave your home when he has obtained an order from the court which tells you to leave. This is known as an order for possession.

When will the court give my landlord an order for possession?

The court will only give your landlord an order for possession when he can prove that your contractual tenancy or your contractual licence has come to an end and that there is a ground or grounds on which the judge can make an order. This is the same procedure as for other regulated tenants in the private sector (see pages 20–24). Your 'contractual' licence or tenancy is the agreement between you and your landlord for you to live in your premises. The 'grounds' for possession relating to agricultural workers are set out in a different statute than those relating to other tenants. Some of the grounds are the same as those available against other private sector tenants. Later in this chapter we will look at the differences.

How does my contractual tenancy come to an end?

If you are a tenant this occurs in the same way as in relation to other private sector tenants (see pages 20–22). If you are a licensee then your right to occupy your premises will come to an end at the end of the 'fixed term' agreed by you and your landlord or can be brought to an end by your employer giving you 'reasonable notice' in the same way as for other licensees in the private sector (see pages 36–38). When your contractual right to occupy your premises comes to an end you will have a 'statutory tenancy' (see page 22). This is so whether you were a tenant or a licensee, see Chaper 15 for your rights in this context.

If you are an agricultural worker, whether a tenant or licensee, and give your landlord a notice to quit this is in certain circumstances a ground for possession in itself and is described later in this chapter.

If my employment ends does my contractual tenancy also come to an end?

No. Your right to occupy your premises is separate from your employment. If you are dismissed or leave your work for another reason this does not mean that you have to leave your premises.

What are the grounds for possession?

The grounds are the facts the landlord must prove to the court before a judge will make an order for possession. The grounds are described in statute as 'cases'. In relation to agricultural occupiers there are thirteen cases in all. In ten of the cases even if the landlord is able to prove the facts to establish that the ground or case is made out he must also prove to the court that it is 'reasonable' to make an order for possession. Reasonable in this context has the same meaning as in possession proceedings against other private sector tenants. See page 24. Where reasonableness must be shown the grounds are called discretionary, because the court has a discretion whether or not to order possession. Where reasonableness is not an element of the case the ground is called mandatory, since once your landlord has proved that the case is applicable to you, the court has no choice but to make an order for possession.

What are the discretionary grounds for possession?

In relation to agricultural occupiers these can be divided into three types: first where alternative accommodation is offered, second where the conduct of the occupier is the basis of the ground, and third where the landlord's needs form the basis of the ground:

1. Alternative Accommodation

Offers of alternative accommodation form the basis of two of the grounds for possession:

(a) The first of these grounds is almost identical to that applicable to ordinary private sector tenants, i.e. that your landlord has offered suitable alternative accommodation to you. If your landlord offers you somewhere else to live it must be 'suitable' in several different respects. It must be big enough for you and your family, near enough to your new place of work, if you have one, and also it must offer a similar degree of security of tenure. This will usually be either an assured or a protected tenancy. Finally, the premises must also be similar to your present accommodation or otherwise suitable as regards 'character'.

(b) The second of these grounds is that alternative accommodation is to be provided or arranged by your local authority. To prove this ground your landlord must show that an offer of suitable accommodation has been made to you by the housing authority concerned, and that you either accepted the offer or unreasonably refused it. The question of whether the accommodation is suitable or not is broadly decided on the same basis as mentioned above.

2. The Occupiers Conduct

This forms the basis of seven of the remaining eight discretionary grounds which are virtually the same as grounds available against other private tenants (see page 25). In the main they can be regarded as cases where the occupier is at fault and are in summary:

(a) Rent arrears or other breach of agreement.

(b) Nuisance or annoyance to adjoining occupiers, for example, by causing too much noise or allowing the premises to be used for illegal or immoral purposes.

(c) Causing damage to the premises.

(d) Causing damage to the furniture provided under the tenancy.

(e) The tenant has given notice to quit (see page 21) and as a result the landlord has made certain arrangements with regard to the premises and would be disadvantaged if he didn't get possession of his property. For example, thinking he was going to get vacant possession he may have agreed to sell the premises.

(f) The tenant has assigned or sublet the whole of his

premises or part of them without his landlord's permission (see also page 100).

(g) The tenant sublet part of the premises and has overcharged rent.

3. The Landlord's Needs

There is only one discretionary ground in this category and it is similar to a ground applicable to other tenants in the private sector (see page 27). The ground is that your landlord reasonably requires your accommodation for a residence for himself, any son or daughter over the age of 18, his father or mother, his father-in-law or mother-in-law, his grandfather, grandmother or his wife/husband's grandfather or grandmother. The requirement for the premises must be reasonable, and this is judged separately from the general question of reasonableness applicable to discretionary grounds (see above and page 24). It also must be the landlord's intention that he or she or one of the relatives will actually live in the premises, as a home, not merely, for example, until the property can be sold.

What are the mandatory grounds for possession?

There are three grounds in this category, the first two again relate to the landlord's needs. They are:

(a) That before the premises were let, the landlord occupied the premises as his home and notified the tenant prior to the tenancy that he may require possession of the premises under this ground and that the landlord now requires the premises once again for his residence.

(b) That the premises were bought as a retirement home and the tenant was notified prior to or at the time of the tenancy that possession may be sought on this ground and either that the landlord has retired and requires the premises as his home or, if the landlord has died, a member of his family who was living with him at the time of his death requires the premises as a home.

When do I have to leave my home if the court makes an order for possession against me?
This depends on what order the court makes against you. The court has power to postpone the date for possession for whatever period it thinks fit. It also has the power in discretionary cases to 'suspend' an order for possession. This means that you are allowed to continue to occupy your home so long as you comply with any conditions the court makes, and that after a specified period the order for possession will no longer apply. For example, if you are in rent arrears but are able to pay those rent arrears off in instalments then the court may make an order for possession which is suspended on the basis that you pay the arrears off at a certain rate and that when the arrears are cleared the order will no longer be applicable (see also page 29).

B. RIGHTS OF OCCUPATION COMMENCING ON OR AFTER 15 JANUARY 1989 – ASSURED AGRICULTURAL OCCUPANCIES

Can my landlord force me to leave my home?
Your landlord can only force you to leave your home when he has obtained an order from the court requiring you to go, known as an order for possession.

When will the court give my landlord an order for possession?
The circumstances in which the court will give your landlord an order for possession are virtually the same as for any other assured tenant in the private sector, see pages 30–34. The main exception to this is that the ground for possession aimed specifically at those who obtained their accommodation as a consequence of their employment (see page 34) is not applicable to you.

15: Agricultural Statutory Tenancies

What is a statutory tenancy?

A statutory tenancy is the term used to describe the right you have to occupy your premises after your contractual tenancy has been brought to an end (see page 22). As far as agricultural workers are concerned, those who are entitled to statutory tenancies are workers whose rights to occupy their premises commenced on or before 15 January 1989 and who qualify for either the protection afforded to other private sector tenants, i.e. protected tenants and those who are protected agricultural occupiers, see pages 81–84. (Those whose right of occupation commenced after 15 January 1989 have no need of the protection of statutory tenancies because of the different nature and procedures in regard to their rights of occupation. See pages 30–34). If you are a protected agricultural occupier and have a licence, you will also be entitled to a statutory tenancy when your licence agreement comes to an end.

What are the terms of my statutory tenancy if I am a protected tenant?

The terms of your statutory tenancy are the same as the terms of your contractual tenancy. This is so for all protected tenants (see page 22 and *The Private Tenants Handbook*).

What are the terms of my statutory tenancy if I am a protected agricultural occupier?

If you are a protected agricultural occupier then, generally speaking, the terms of your statutory tenancy will be the same as the terms of your contractual tenancy. However, certain rights and obligations are specified in statute as being applicable to agricultural statutory tenancies, and will apply whether your original agreement was a tenancy *or* a licence. The most important of these are: that your landlord should allow you quiet enjoyment of your premises, that your landlord should repair the premises, and that you should use the premises in a tenant-like manner. These terms are all implied into tenancies generally and are fully explained in *The Private Tenants Handbook*;

Quiet enjoyment: the right not to be unduly interfered with by your landlord in the occupation of your accommodation.

Repairs: that your landlord must carry out repairs to the structure and exterior of your accommodation and to the installations for gas, water and electricity (and see Chapter 20).

Tenant-like manner: this means that you must take proper care of your accommodation, for example turn off the water if you go away in the winter, clear drains and generally do the minor jobs around the place that any reasonable tenant would do.

Is there any change in my rent when I become a statutory agricultural occupier?

At the stage you become a statutory agricultural occupier there may be a change in your rent. This is dealt with on page 98.

16: Other Agricultural Occupiers – Security of Tenure

Do all agricultural occupiers who do not qualify for special protection have the same security of tenure?

No. As we saw in Chapter 13, your status is determined initially on the general principles relating to the private sector. If you are not a protected agricultural occupier the extent of your security of tenure will depend initially on whether you are a tenant or a licensee and the considerations in relation to other occupiers in the private sector set out on page 13 will apply to you. You may be a tenant with the same protection as protected or assured tenants, a no-rent tenant attracting lesser protection than others in the private sector, a service occupier or a licensee on general principles. Additionally, if you work in agriculture your rights as a service occupier may be greater than others in the private sector and you will be referred to as an agricultural service occupier. In this chapter we will examine the security of tenure of these remaining categories.

What is my security of tenure if I am a protected or assured tenant?

Your security of tenure will be at least as good as any other protected or assured tenant. As with other protected or assured tenants your security varies depending on whether your tenancy commenced before or after 15 January 1989.

A. TENANCIES COMMENCING BEFORE 15 JANUARY 1989 (PROTECTED TENANCIES)

When will the court give my landlord an order for possession?

The court will give your landlord an order for possession on the same principles and in the same way as for other private sector tenants, see pages 23–30.

If you fit into the category of tenants who would have qualified as a protected agricultural occupier if you had been paying a low rent then you are given the equivalent and additional rights afforded to protected agricultural occupiers dealt with in the last chapter. The point of this is that you are not penalized in respect to your rights just because you pay a proper rent. In order to qualify for the special rights given to agricultural occupiers, however, you must fulfil the other conditions set out on pages 81–84, i.e. your accommodation must be in qualifying ownership, and you must be a qualifying worker. If you do fulfil these conditions then your rights as a protected tenant are varied as follows:

(a) All of the discretionary grounds for possession (that is the grounds which require the court to consider the question of reasonableness, see pages 24–25) are available to a landlord against you *except* for the case specifically aimed at service tenants and dealt with on page 27.

(b) All of the mandatory grounds are available against you *except* three grounds which deal with the regaining of possession of premises for other agricultural workers. The point of this is that those grounds which would usually be available against private sector tenants for the benefit of agricultural workers are not to be used against agricultural workers themselves.

(c) The two grounds based on offers of suitable alternative accommodation dealt with on page 87 will be available against you.

B. TENANCIES COMMENCING ON OR AFTER 15 JANUARY 1989 (ASSURED TENANCIES)

When will the court give my landlord an order for possession?

The court will give your landlord an order for possession in the same circumstances as for other assured tenants, as those rights are adapted for assured agricultural occupancies. See pages 31 and 90 and *The Private Tenants Handbook*.

What is my security of tenure if I am an agricultural service occupier?

In order to be able to evict you, your landlord must obtain an order from court. Once your landlord has terminated your right to occupy your premises (see page 36), he may apply to a court for an order against you without having to prove any reason or ground for the court to grant possession. However, the court has additional powers over and above its usual powers to delay possession. The power is to delay the operation of an order for possession for any period that the judge thinks is reasonable. In practice this period is usually between four to six weeks unless the possession order is made within six months of your right of occupation coming to an end, when the court *must* suspend the operation of the order until the end of that six months.

In deciding what is a reasonable period to postpone the order for possession, the judge must take account of:

(a) whether other suitable accommodation is or can be made available to you,

(b) whether the efficient management of your landlord's business would be prejudiced if your home was not available for him to put to use, and

(c) the hardship that would be caused to either you or your landlord if the order were suspended or not.

In an exceptional case the court may order possession of your premises prior to the end of the six months. In such a case the judge would also consider the question of whether you or anyone living with you had caused damage to the premises rented to you.

What is my security of tenure if I am not even an 'agricultural service occupier'?

If you do not even qualify under the definition of agricultural service occupier (see page 80), then your rights will be limited to those of any other unprotected tenant or licensee in the private sector (see pages 35–36). In particular you will not qualify for the special powers the court has to suspend an order for possession mentioned in the last paragraph.

17: Agricultural Workers – Rents

What rent must I pay to my landlord?
Initially the amount of rent you must pay your landlord, whatever type of agricultural occupier you are, is the amount which was agreed when you first moved into the premises. Many agricultural occupiers pay no rent at all. The money you pay may include service charges, and sometimes a contribution towards bills.

Do all agricultural workers have the same rights in relation to rent?
No. There are different rules governing the rights of the different categories of agricultural workers. Your rights will differ depending on whether you are an occupier with the same rights as protected or assured tenants in the private sector, or whether you are a protected agricultural occupier, or a service occupier. If you are a protected or assured tenant your rights are those set out on pages 42–49; if you are a service occupier your rights are the same as those set out on pages 40–42. The remaining category of protected agricultural occupiers are dealt with in this chapter.

A. PROTECTED AGRICULTURAL OCCUPIERS

Are the rights of all protected agricultural occupiers the same in regard to rent?
No. The rules relating to rent in respect of protected agricultural occupancies differ depending on whether your right of occupation commenced before 15 January

1989 or on or after that date, i.e. on whether you have a protected occupancy or an assured agricultural occupancy.

1. Protected Occupancies

Are there controls on the rents that can be charged to protected occupiers?
Yes. Those controls are very similar to the controls applicable to protected tenants in the private sector, in particular the system of rent registration applies to protected occupancies as it does to protected tenants. See page 43. However, there are some extra controls. It is necessary in order to understand these controls to look at the period when your original agreement for occupation is still in existence separately from the period when it has been terminated and you have become an agricultural statutory tenant (see page 91).

Can my landlord put my rent up before the original agreement for my accommodation has been brought to an end?
No, unless it was a term of that agreement that the rent could be varied. For example you may have agreed that your rent could be increased once a year by a certain percentage.

What happens when the original agreement comes to an end?
When the original agreement comes to an end, you and your landlord should come to a specific agreement about how much rent will be paid, or that no rent should be paid. If you do agree on a rent it should not be more than any registered rent (see page 43) for the property if there is one. If there is no registered rent it should not be more than one-and-a-half times the rateable value of the prop-

erty, or if this occurs after 31 March 1990 the usual annual rent for that type of property. If a rent is registered after you have come to an agreement and it is less than the agreed amount, then the proper amount of rent is the registered rent and not the agreed rent.

If your landlord tries to charge you more than the registered rent or more than the amount set out on page 98, you may refuse to pay the excess and your landlord will not be able to sue you for that amount.

Can an agreement for a rent for a statutory tenancy be varied?

Yes. As long as the new amount doesn't exceed the registered rent or more than the amount set out on page 98. A variation may be achieved by an agreement between you and your landlord, or by your landlord giving notice that the last agreement is to be terminated and a separate notice in a specified form that your rent is to be increased.

If I have overpaid rent, can I get any excess payment back?

Yes, if you have overpaid rent you can recover that overpayment as far back as two years by either deducting the total sum from future rent payments or by going to court. If you decide to deduct money from future rent payments you should be very certain of your ground and notify your landlord of what you are going to do in advance. If you are in doubt, you should consult an advice agency or a solicitor.

2. Assured Agricultural Occupancies

Are there controls on the rents that can be charged to assured agricultural occupants?

Yes, those controls are the same as the controls applicable to assured tenants and you should see pages 47–49 for your rights.

18: Agricultural Workers – Sharing

Am I allowed to share my home?
Yes. You are in the same position as others in the private sector and should see Chapter 6 for your rights in this respect. The rules relating to succession on death relating to agricultural workers are dealt with separately here.

Do all agricultural workers have the same rights in relation to succession to their accommodation?
No. The rights of your family to succeed to your tenancy on your death vary depending on what class of occupant you are. If you are a protected or assured tenant then your rights are the same as either category and are dealt with on pages 53–54. If you are a protected agricultural occupier your rights will be dealt with in this chapter. If you are a no-rent tenant you do have the right to pass on your tenancy but given your limited security such a tenancy would be of little value. If you are a service occupant you have no right to pass on your tenancy.

What rights of succession are there for protected agricultural occupiers?
On your death either your spouse or another member of your family can take over the tenancy. Only a spouse who was living at the premises at the time of the tenant's death qualifies – but takes precedence over any other member of the tenant's family.

If you are not actually married to your partner but have been cohabiting for years in a stable enough relationship to be regarded as a 'common-law spouse' then when you die your partner will be able to inherit from you as long as you were living together at the time of death.

If no spouse or common-law spouse were residing with you at the time of your death then another member of your family may be able to inherit. To qualify, the member of the family would have had to have been living with you for a specified period. If your right of occupation commenced before 15 January 1989 the period is six months, if after that date the period is two years.

There is no fixed rule as to who fits into the category of 'member of the family'; it can include children, brothers and sisters, etc., but also step-relationships, in-law relationships, etc. may qualify.

If there is more than one potential successor then the question of who should succeed may be decided by agreement among the potential successors, or if you are unable to agree, the question can be referred to the court to decide.

19: Homelessness

Do I have any rights to be rehoused if I am evicted?

If you are evicted you may have the right to apply to your local authority for housing. For a detailed answer to this question you should see *The Homeless Persons Handbook* in this series. You may at any time apply to go on to your local authority's housing list. In certain circumstances you may be entitled to be rehoused immediately without the long wait usually involved in being housed from the list. Basically in order to be rehoused you must have a 'priority need' for housing and it must not be your own fault that you are homeless.

Do I actually have to be on the streets before I am regarded as being homeless?

No. If you are in accommodation in which you have no legal right to be, or if you have moved to accommodation on a temporary basis and are threatened with homelessness in 28 days, then you will be regarded as being homeless for the purposes of the local authority's duty towards you. For example, if a court has made an order for possession against you, but has agreed that it should not take effect for four weeks, then your local authority should consider any application for housing you make immediately.

Do I have a priority need for housing?

You have a priority need for housing if you have young children, if you or your spouse or co-habitee is pregnant, if you are over retirement age or if you are in some other way vulnerable so that you would have difficulty in obtaining accommodation without your local authority's assistance.

What difference does it make if I have made myself homeless?

If you have made yourself homeless, for example by leaving accommodation which you could reasonably have stayed in, then your local authority is entitled to refuse to rehouse you. In fact this is quite a complex question, but as a basic guide if you leave accommodation for no good reason or are forced to leave accommodation because of something you have done, for example building up rent arrears for no good reason or causing a nuisance, you may be regarded as being intentionally homeless. Not everyone who is forced to leave accommodation by an order of court is intentionally homeless; for example if you are a service occupier or a residential occupier then once your landlord applies to court for an order for possession, as we have seen, the court has no choice but to give him that order. Having said this, if the reason you have lost your tied accommodation is that you have been dismissed from your work because of your own misbehaviour, then it can be said that you lost your accommodation through your own actions and fault and you may be intentionally homeless.

In those circumstances you are not necessarily at fault, and may be entitled to be rehoused. While your local authority is making inquiries into whether or not you have made yourself homeless intentionally you will be housed in some sort of temporary accommodation.

What sort of accommodation will I be given by my local authority?

Once your local authority has accepted that it should rehouse you, you will probably at first be given some sort of temporary accommodation such as bed and breakfast until a property which is suitable to your needs becomes available. When you are offered permanent accommodation it may not be entirely to your liking but, unless there is something very wrong or very unsuitable about the accommodation, your authority will have discharged its duty towards you and will not be obliged to offer you anywhere else.

Will I get any assistance if I am not in priority need?

Although there is no duty on your local authority to rehouse you, some authorities do have schemes to house, for example, the single homeless, and also they should give you advice and assistance in finding accommodation for yourself.

Will I get any assistance if I have made myself homeless?

If you are in priority need but have made yourself homeless then your local authority will allow you to remain in temporary accommodation or give you temporary accommodation for a short period, usually about 28 days, in order to give you some breathing space to find somewhere to move to.

Can I do anything if my local authority makes a decision that I do not agree with?

Yes. Sometimes local authorities have an internal appeal procedure and if so this procedure should be followed first. If not, or once that has been exhausted, a challenge can be made to the decision by court proceedings known as 'judicial review'. These proceedings are complicated and have strict time limits, therefore if you find yourself in a position where you wish to challenge your local authority you should go immediately to a solicitor or a law centre for advice and assistance.

20: Repairs

As a tied occupier can I force my landlord to carry out repairs to my accommodation?

Yes, but the extent to which you can do this varies according to which category of tied occupier you are. The basic distinction is between tenants and licensees. Those who are tenants include those who have been described in this book as protected tenants, service tenants (and secure licensees who we have seen are treated in the same way as secure tenants, see page 61), secure service tenants, and agricultural tenants. Licensees mentioned in this book include service occupiers and other licensees, but where repairs are concerned note the special provision for protected agricultural workers who have become statutory tenants (see page 91), and have the same rights to have their homes repaired as tenants. Residential occupiers have the same rights to repairs as secure tenants.

A. TENANTS

What rights do tenants have to force their landlords to carry out repairs to their accommodation?

Tenants in tied accommodation have the same rights to have repairs carried out as any other tenants in the private or public sector.

Who is responsible for repairs?

Your landlord is responsible for major repairs unless your tenancy is for more than seven years or it commenced before 24 October 1961. This is so no matter what your tenancy agreement says.

Major repairs include the structure and exterior of the property. In a flat this includes the outside walls of the flat or room, the floor and the floor above the ceiling, the window frames and fittings. In a house it includes the walls, floors, ceilings, roof, windows, etc. It does not include internal decoration or minor internal repairs. However if the state of the interior is damaged for example by damp, then the landlord may have to put the interior back into proper condition. Major repairs also include repair and maintenance of the installations for heating and gas, electricity and water supplies including basins, sinks and lavatories. It does not include, for example, your own cooker, refrigerator or other installations.

If you live in a flat then there is a duty on your landlord to keep the 'common parts' of the building in acceptable condition and in particular in a condition that they do not cause damage to you, your property or your visitors. Common parts include halls, stairs, corridors, the front door and also the parts of the structure of the building that are not included in your tenancy such as, in some cases, the roof.

You are responsible for minor repairs and internal redecoration and also you are obliged to 'use the premises in a tenant-like manner', this means you must use the property reasonably and take reasonable care of it; for example, unblocking the sink, mending fuses, cleaning windows, etc. Of course normal wear and tear is to be expected and if the property deteriorates to a state of disrepair because of normal usage it then becomes a matter for your landlord to put right.

Whose responsibility is it to find out about disrepair?

To a large extent yours. Your landlord is not under an obligation to carry out repairs until he knows about them and since you are living in the premises you are the most likely person to discover them. If and when you discover something wrong with your home you should tell your landlord about it, or preferably put your complaint in writing and keep a copy of the letter. The notice to your landlord need not come from you; for example, the landlord or his agent may have inspected the property, or a neighbour may have complained or the local authority may have inspected on your behalf and served notice on your landlord to carry out repairs.

Does my landlord have to carry out repairs within a specified period?

Once your landlord has been notified that there is disrepair he has a 'reasonable period' in which to put matters right. What a reasonable period is depends on what the disrepair is; for example, if your landlord has to carry out major structural repairs to remedy penetrating dampness, the time he should be allowed is longer than if your complaint is more minor such as a leaking cistern which can be dealt with on one visit by a plumber. In general, however, a reasonable period will include the time it takes to arrange for workmen or in a serious case a surveyor to come and look at the problem, plus a period of time to allow workmen to come to the premises, plus the time it takes to carry out the repair.

Must I allow my landlord access to my home to carry out repairs?

Yes. It is a part of every tenancy agreement that access should be allowed to your landlord both to inspect as to the state of repair and to carry out repairs.

This right does not include the right to inspect for and carry out improvements. If you do not agree to improvements being carried out you do not have to give access to your landlord. In some cases, however, where your landlord has obtained grant aid, he can apply to the court to give him an order that you grant him access. In this case the court may make provision to accommodate your needs whilst improvement works are carried out, and in some cases will order that you be provided with alternative accommodation.

Does my landlord have to provide me with alternative accommodation while he carries out repairs?
No. But if you have to move out of the premises for a lengthy period whilst works are carried out, you may be able to claim the reasonable cost of alternative accommodation as damages.

What can I do if my landlord refuses to carry out repairs?
If your landlord has had notice of disrepair and after a reasonable period has not carried out any remedial works then you can take him to court to get an order that he carries out repairs.

If you have been living in premises which have been in disrepair for a lengthy period you can also claim damages for the inconvenience and distress caused by your landlord's default. You will also be able to claim for any property which has been damaged as a result of the disrepair.

An alternative course of action is to inform the local authority's Environmental Health Department, who will inspect and if appropriate serve a notice on your landlord requiring him to carry out the work.

B. LICENSEES

Who is responsible for keeping the premises in a state of repair?

In general the obligation is on the landlord to keep the premises in a condition fit for the purpose for which they were let; that means in a condition fit to live in. This would include, for example, keeping the roof, walls and windows in such a state of repair that the property is wind and water tight. Also you may have agreed either orally or in writing that your landlord would carry out repairs.

As a licensee you can be expected not to damage the property, but there is not usually any obligation on you to carry out internal repairs, unless there is a complimentary agreement that your landlord will carry out external repairs.

Whose responsibility is it to find out about disrepair?

In theory the burden of finding out about disrepair falls more heavily on your landlord than in the case of tenancies. However, it is a matter of common sense that if you know there is something wrong with your premises you should inform your landlord of this.

Can I force my landlord to carry out repairs?

Yes, you can either take your landlord to court, or you can inform the local authority about the state of your premises. However, as a licensee you should be careful how you deal with your landlord since you have very limited security of tenure and any extreme action on your part may prompt retaliatory possession proceedings by your landlord.

C. ALL OCCUPIERS

Do I have rights in respect of repairs other than those included in the agreement with my landlord?
Yes. Your local authority has wide powers in respect of rented premises and can force your landlord to carry out repairs to the property in which you live whether you are a licensee or a tenant.

When can the local authority force my landlord to repair?
There are two main sets of circumstances where a local authority can take action against your landlord.

(a) Your local authority may take criminal proceedings against your landlord where the premises are in such a state of disrepair that they constitute a 'statutory nuisance'. This means either that the premises are in such a state that there is a risk to your health, or to that of any other occupant, or that there is a defect in the common parts or neighbouring premises under the landlord's control which is causing harm to your premises.

You may initiate criminal proceedings yourself. In particular this is useful where you are a public sector occupier. If contemplating this course of action, it would be sensible to take legal advice.

(b) Your local authority may also take action in respect of the following:

(i) Unfitness for human habitation: this means that the premises are so defective in relation to one or more of the following matters that they are not reasonably suitable for occupation in that condition: repairs, stability, freedom from damp, internal arrangement (such as steep or insecure stairs), natural lighting, ventilation, water supply, drainage, and facilities for preparing and cooking food and for disposing of waste water.

(ii) Serious disrepair (designed to prevent premises becoming unfit for human habitation).

(iii) Conditions such as might interfere with your personal comfort (such as dangerous wiring, dampness enough to be prejudicial to your health, or to qualify the premises as unfit for human habitation).

In these cases the local authority has a variety of powers ranging from notices requiring works to be carried out, and powers to carry out works in default of compliance, to the power to close premises, i.e. prevent occupation of them.